ALSO BY JOHN V. DENNIS

A Complete Guide to Bird Feeding (1975)

*with Dr. C. R. Gunn*
World Guide to Tropical Drift Seeds and Fruits (1976)

# Beyond the Bird Feeder

# Beyond the Bird Feeder

*The habits and behavior of feeding-station birds
when they are not at your feeder*

## John V. Dennis

*Drawings by Matthew Kalmenoff*

 ALFRED A. KNOPF   NEW YORK   1981

Library of Congress Cataloging in Publication Data

Dennis, John V.
Beyond the bird feeder.
Includes index.
1. Birds—Behavior.   I. Title.
QL698.3.D46     1981     598.2′51     81–47491
ISBN 0–394–50890–4          AACR2

*for my wife, Mary Alice*

# Contents

# Preface

When I was writing *A Complete Guide to Bird Feeding,* my editor at Knopf, Angus Cameron, suggested that I should write more about birds when they were away from the feeder. I knew from long experience that birds were much less cooperative in revealing their ways after they leave our grounds. They become more wary. Only with the greatest difficulty can one pick up the same behavior patterns in the wild that birds reveal so freely when they are in our yards.

As it turned out, Angus and I had a communication problem. He didn't mean literally that I had to creep on all fours through the underbrush in order to spy upon birds after they had left the feeder. All he wanted was a broad view of the habits and behavior of birds, broader than I could obtain if I had confined my observations to the bird feeder. I could still watch the bird feeder for the wealth of events that take place there; at the same time, I mustn't neglect other opportunities wherever they might occur. I could go beyond the bird feeder, far beyond if I wished.

By the time I had finished my bird-feeding guide, which did include beyond-the-feeder observations, Angus's message had sifted through my cranium. There was still room for more, many more, observations on the habits and behavior of feeding-station birds. Obviously I must write another book. This one I would call *Beyond the Bird Feeder* and in it I would include observations of feeding-station birds wherever they might be.

My aim is to show that there are new frontiers open to anyone who will watch and learn. So many of the smallest actions of birds have their significance. Putting together the pieces, as in a jigsaw puzzle, leads to new interpretations of bird behavior. This is a field where the amateur is constantly making contributions. You, your yard, and your birds can become involved. If only for your own enjoyment, it will be a rewarding experience to begin watching birds more closely and following them beyond the bird feeder.

In the first chapter, I begin my safari by looking into that most incredible of all bird performances—migration. How birds twice-yearly make their way to tiny targets with uncanny accuracy taxes the imagination. When we stop to think of it, our yard, however small, is the goal of both birds that come to nest and birds that arrive to spend the winter. Although migration is largely an unseen phenomenon, we can obtain an inkling of what is taking place even in the city. There will be arrivals, departures, busy days at the feeder and birdbath, empty days, and call notes overhead on starry nights. For migrants at their winter homes in the tropics, I go to Central America and the West Indies. Amid an entirely different setting and surrounded by strange birds, our migrants conduct their lives much as before. A few even find hospitality at bird feeders.

I was afraid that nesting habits would take me too far from the focal point of my book, which is still the bird feeding station. So, aside from a few references to courtship and protection of the nest, I leave this side of bird study to others. Anyone interested in full accounts of the nesting habits of North American birds should consult A. C. Bent's *Life Histories*.

Food is a topic much closer to my theme. In my next chapter, I revisit the bird feeder and, at the same time, do not overlook feeding habits in the wild. Beyond the range of our immediate influence, birds give a truer picture of the way they react to that most basic of all drives—hunger. They find food by remembering shape and color. They also startle us by showing great precision in locating food that has become buried deep under snow or covered by earth.

Water deserved a chapter. This essential ingredient is used by birds for bathing and drinking. It is as important to them in winter as it is in summer. The birdbath is the neglected opportunity that awaits all who would delve more deeply into bird habits and behavior. When coming to water, birds reveal a side that we do not see anywhere else.

Paralleling water in importance is other bathing, including sunbathing, bathing in dust, smoke, and, strangest of all, the secretions of ants. How birds take ants and rub them in their plumage is the main topic of my next chapter. Anting, as it is called, is one of the least observed and understood of all actions indulged in by birds. We may be fortunate enough to see examples of this strange performance in our yards. There is good reason to believe that a relationship exists between anting and the discomfort that birds suffer during the molt period.

In the chapter that follows, on how birds elude their enemies, I report upon a number of stratagems, including mobbing and sudden departures from the feeding station. Birds are constantly alert to danger. They warn each other of an approaching predator and join forces to drive it away or keep it under surveillance. They find more safety in numbers than going it alone.

In chapter 6, I tell of some of the high-handed tactics birds use in obtaining their daily rations. They at times bully, rob, and drive off other birds. But unruly behavior is the exception, not the rule. For the most part, birds settle their differences peacefully. They recognize which members of the flock have priority at food, water, or roosting sites. By knowing their places in the "peck order," birds avoid serious conflicts and share with one another with a minimum of friction. If they can do this so successfully, why can't we?

I somehow couldn't overlook the importance of habitat in this book. In a chapter on this subject, I tell of my experience in transplanting wild plants from the fencerow to my yard. Since these were plants that owed their existence to birds, I felt that I could hardly go wrong from a bird-attracting standpoint. Moreover, many of the plants were valuable ornamentals. I also recommend a number of good bird-food plants that can be obtained at nurseries. With the fruits and berries of such plants, with feeding-station fare, and with the extra provision of sap provided by sapsuckers, I have few hungry customers. Sapsucker drillings in trees constitute the first bird-feeding stations. Many birds besides sapsuckers come to these sap wells for liquid refreshment.

Weather, like habitat, as I point out in my next chapter, is a factor in deciding how well our yard will be patronized by birds. Rain, snow, wind, and temperature differences, for example, have an important bearing upon attendance at the feeding station. While it is true that birds are sometimes at the mercy of the weather, they surprise us by reacting in ways different from what we would expect. Cold, icy winds from the north, along with snow, may simply lend zest to the feeding activities of some of our birds. Snow helps birds in a number of ways, including making some foods more visible. But there are times when the weather is so bad that all birds suffer. I illustrate this by referring to our hard winters and Britain's disastrously cold winter of 1962–1963.

Finally, in the last chapter, the house itself is the stage for strange doings by birds. Window panes elicit certain responses from birds and chimneys still others. The interior of the house has not escaped the attention of birds either. In England birds sometimes invade the interior, with devastating results. Our own birds might do the same if they weren't largely frustrated by screens and closed windows. Another bird habit that can be troublesome is eating fresh putty at edges of window panes. In spite of minor problems like these, I urge more nesting sites for birds on and near houses. If we take a little trouble, we generally end up with a better class of tenants.

Besides being indebted to Angus Cameron for having initiated the original idea for this book, I am grateful to my present editors, Jane Garrett and Barbara Bristol, for their help and inspiration. Again, for his superb illustrations, I owe a debt of gratitude to Matthew Kalmenoff. Without slighting, I hope, the many persons who have supplied help and information, for which I am truly grateful, I feel I must limit special acknowledgments to those who have read portions of the manuscript and offered comments. For their help in this regard, I am grateful to Aelred D. Geis, Cedric M. Smith, Robert W. Sampson, John S. Weske, Charles Vaughn, Eloise Potter, Jean Bancroft, and Kathryn Clay.

# Autobiographical Note

Those of us who watch birds often establish territories for ourselves. These are not territories in the sense of excluding trespassers. Rather they are well-defined areas where we pay particular attention to the birdlife and perhaps other animal life and plantlife as well. As an early example of establishment of territory, I need only mention the eighteenth-century curate, Gilbert White, who wrote so delightfully about the birds and other animals of Selbourne in England. On this side of the Atlantic, we have our Thoreau and his Walden Pond.

In contrast, the present-day naturalist or bird watcher is much more likely to be on the go. He picks a territory wherever he happens to stay long enough to focus his binoculars. This has been very much the case with me. I couldn't begin to list the many territories I have established for myself in the course of my travels. The places I remember best, however, are those where I've fed birds. These are the places that figure most importantly in this book.

Beginning with my Maryland bird feeders, I should explain that I am speaking of a part of Maryland that remained little known and obscure until the advent of James Michener's best-selling *Chesapeake*. This is the Eastern Shore of Maryland situated between the Atlantic Ocean and Chesapeake Bay. Low-lying and marshy, the Shore, as it is called, is a mecca for waterfowl, while the human inhabitants are independent-minded people who, for the most part, have always made their livelihoods from the land and water. But the Eastern Shoreman is far more peaceful and law-abiding than Michener would have us believe; in fact, over the long period of time since the first settlers arrived, the Shore has remained outside the mainstream of events. It is a backwater where little ever happens.

During a childhood spent on the Shore, I obtained an introduction to birds and other animal life through the kindly tutelage of my grandfather. But from college days until a few years ago, I saw little of the Shore. Nevertheless the attractions of water, marsh, and the memory of piercing screams of the osprey remained strong. With my wife, Mary Alice, I came back to the very town where I was born and where the Dennis family has roots going back to the seventeenth century. I must give credit to the bird feeders and grounds of our house in the small town of Princess Anne for many of the observations that appear in this book.

If anything, equal credit must be given to my Massachusetts bird feeders. After serving with the U. S. Army Signal Corps in India and China during World War II, I worked briefly at a federal waterfowl refuge in Louisiana and then moved to Massachusetts to take a job with the Massachusetts Audubon Society. This was a turning point in my life. For the first time, I met people who talked, breathed, and lived for birds. Although I may have expressed their dedication a little too strongly, it was the influence of my Massachusetts friends that made a life-long birdman out of me. As director of the Society's Moose Hill Bird Sanctuary at Sharon, near Boston, I learned most of what I know about feeding birds and banding them.

Bird feeding and birdbanding go hand in hand. You lure birds into traps baited with either food or water. The numbered leg band you give the bird helps the bander keep track of it during its lifetime. The dead bird with a band on its leg is an equally important source of scientific data. Whether recovered dead or alive, the banded bird tells us something about the life span of birds and their travels. Without the intimate acquaintanceship I've had with birds through years of feeding and banding them, I almost certainly couldn't have written this book.

Bird listing also attracted my interest during my Massachusetts sojourn. This is a competitive game to see how many different bird species one can find in a year or in a given area. The dean of this sport, whose ability and opinion was respected by everyone, was Ludlow Griscom, who was with the

Museum of Comparative Zoology at Harvard. Whenever I encountered him on field trips, I was impressed by his ability to identify birds so far away that no one else could see them. Never very proficient at picking up rarities, I gravitated toward the common birds, finding them easier to study and more interesting. I should hasten to say that I have always made an exception of rare woodpeckers. I have made many a trip to the South in search of the nearly extinct ivory-billed woodpecker or to become better acquainted with the rare red-cockaded woodpecker of southern pinelands. I've had a certain amount of success with both species, but this is a different story entirely from the one at hand.

While Moose Hill was the starting point in my bird-feeding career, the island of Nantucket, not so far away, has been the scene of more bird banding and bird feeding by me than perhaps any other place I've lived. I owe my introduction to Nantucket to my wife, Mary Alice. She spent part of her girlhood on the island and this is where we have spent much of our time since our marriage at the end of 1945. For several years I ran a bird-banding station on the island. In recent years we have established the routine of spending the summer and part of the spring and fall at our home on Nantucket and the rest of the year on the Eastern Shore.

I shouldn't overlook Florida as another state where bird feeding has figured importantly in my life. In 1949, I left the Massachusetts Audubon Society to enter graduate school at the University of Florida in Gainesville. By now we had two small children, a girl and a boy. It wasn't easy being a student and a father at the same time. Nevertheless I enjoyed my course work, which led to a masters degree in ornithology, and found time to continue my bird feeding and bird-banding.

A period of years living on a farm in Virginia was perhaps the most fruitful time of any from the standpoint of obtaining information for this book. For approximately ten years, beginning in 1952, we lived on a farm at the edge of the Potomac River and near the town of Leesburg. During part of this time, I tried my hand first at dairy farming and then at raising beef cattle. But like Audubon, I wasn't cut out for farming or business. I tended to spend much more time on birds.

Various assignments pertaining to wildlife or preserving natural areas have taken me to South Carolina, to my way of thinking one of the most beautiful and unspoiled of the southern states. I've fed birds at several of the coastal resort areas north of Charleston and always obtained a ready response. This is one of the pleasures of bird feeding—it can be practiced anywhere and at any season. Even in the West Indies, where I've viewed bird feeding in Trinidad, Tobago, and Jamaica, birds are as eager for food offerings as they are anywhere in this country. The same can be said of the birds in Costa Rica in Central America.

If there is any part of the world where people are more attached to bird feeding than on this continent, it is the British Isles. Ever since our daughter and her family moved to England some years ago, we have had a good excuse to visit this country with its rich birdlife and friendly people. I am always impressed with how tame and sometimes impertinent the British birds are. They have perhaps responded a little too well to bird feeding. Nevertheless their antics provide a never-ending source of entertainment.

Should anyone ask me if I ever tire of watching the birds at my feeder, I would emphatically say *no*. No two seasons or even two days at the bird feeder are the same. There is always something new and different happening. There is so much happening every time I look out my windows that I have felt compelled to go a step farther this time and look beyond the immediate confines of the bird feeder. I hope readers will find this world as exciting and interesting as I have.

# Beyond the Bird Feeder

# Migration and Bird Feeding | 1

Overhead on clear autumn nights come faint call notes that echo the unseen movement of birds on their way to winter homes that may lie hundreds or thousands of miles to the south of us. Some are going no farther than our middle or southern states, while others are making spectacular journeys to the tropics. By day these intrepid flyers rest and feed, sometimes swarming in tree-tops or coming lower, depending somewhat upon circumstances. If it is a clear night with northerly winds, the movement will get underway again.

Sometimes the city is the best place to observe migration. In New York City there are days in the fall when parts of Central Park are teeming with small land bird migrants. The same kind of inundations also take place in the spring as migrants head northward. The smallest city yard may draw enough migrants to provide excitement. In an article in a 1975 issue of *Maryland Birdlife*, Peggy Bohanan tells of compiling a list of 105 bird species in a city block in the heart of downtown Baltimore. The few small yards within the block served as an oasis amid surrounding brick and concrete. Similar results were obtained in a small yard in Brooklyn where, by coincidence, 105 species were recorded over a period of several migration seasons.

City dwellers are sometimes reminded of the hazards of migration when they find bodies of warblers and other birds lying on streets and pavements. These birds are victims of unfavorable weather such as a low ceiling, which may act to force nocturnal migrants toward the ground. On such nights large numbers of migrants may hit TV towers, tall buildings, and bridges. It is too bad that we can't somehow warn birds of these dangers.

Beginning with shorebirds in early July and ending with sparrows and finches in November, migration southward takes place over a five-month period. The peak period for movement is in September and early October. For those summer residents that nest in our yards and return south, it is a relatively short sojourn. Many begin leaving in August, and by mid-September most will have departed. The unseen departures will leave gaps in our home bird population. Also in late summer, many birds that we regard as permanent residents are drifting away. Some will have gone no farther than a neighbor's yard; others, especially young-of-the-year, more venturesome and perhaps seeking new homes, will fly many miles. All birds, regardless of how far they will go, are now coming under the grip of migratory restlessness. The cares of the nesting season over and natural food supplies plentiful, there is no longer a need to stay so close to home.

The effects of the fall exodus are becoming apparent at the feeding station. With so many departures attendance has now reached its lowest level of the year. The migrants that sometimes appear in the yard at this time of the year are seldom attracted by food offerings. Insects, fruits, and berries may detain them briefly, while *water* is a major attraction.

Late summer hasn't completely emptied our bird feeders. Birds we care less about have a habit of staying on and on, while a few old standbys, with impeccable reputations, still honor us with their presence. The starlings, grackles, and cowbirds that, in spite of little reciprocation on our part, still cling to our premises will be likely to leave in another month. Not so obliging are house sparrows, which like the poor, are always with us. However, this imprudent import from Europe is disappearing in many areas and is being replaced by the much more popular house finch. The few woodpeckers, nuthatches, titmice (including chickadees), and cardinals that still visit our feeders during this

*Fall migrants winging their way southward in
the night skies above a large city*

slack time of the year remind us that maybe we shouldn't discontinue feeding after all. There may be loyal customers, like the white-breasted nuthatch in Lexington, Massachusetts, that in over a year never missed a day at the feeder, except for a week in June. Devotion such as this deserves its reward. We may also decide that keeping a few birds in residence will ensure better results later on when birds begin to establish winter feeding territories.

As September passes into October, there will still be many clear nights when throngs of birds are passing overhead. Lower temperature, as well as shorter daylight hours, are reminders that the impulse to migrate must be obeyed soon. If, perhaps because of psychological reasons or a physical disability, a bird delays too long, the urge to migrate dies. The bird is left to fend for itself wherever it happens to be. Before the advent of feeding stations, the fate of the tardy migrant was usually sealed as soon as cold and snow set in. Now nursed along with the help of feeding stations, the oriole, tanager, or warbler, which normally spends the winter in the tropics, does almost as well if it is our guest; that is, unless the northern winter is too severe.

Still to be resolved is the question of whether any of these stay-behinds that survive the winter breed and produce offspring that also will not migrate. We know through banding that the same northern orioles return to the same feeding stations winter after winter. For a while it looked as though a non-migratory population of northern orioles had come into being. Feeding stations from New England and the Great Lakes southward were playing host to hundreds if not thousands of orioles that were no longer making the long flight to the American tropics. That these birds are vulnerable to hard winters was seen in a drastic reduction in their numbers caused by the bitter cold of 1977 and 1978. For this species a return to the tropics for the winter seems to be the best assurance of survival after all. Could there be a more telling example of the importance of migration?

Returning to early fall's scarcity, we wonder how long the birds we most count upon will be absent from the feeding station. Is there any way to foretell the return of small woodpeckers, titmice, and nuthatches? And what of the birds that should be arriving from the north to spend the winter with us? When will they be making their appearance?

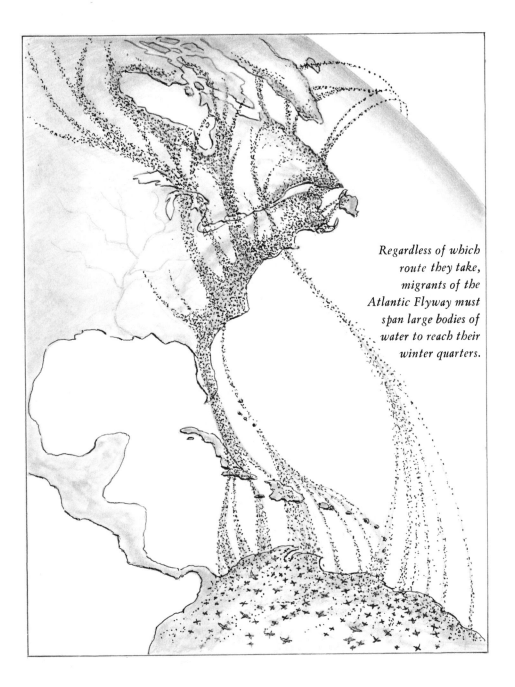

*Regardless of which route they take, migrants of the Atlantic Flyway must span large bodies of water to reach their winter quarters.*

The answers to these questions depend a great deal upon where we live. In the deep South, including Texas and the Southwest, there is not nearly as much turnover in the bird population as there is farther north. There are fewer departures for the tropics and fewer birds arriving from the north. The low point in feeding-station activity for the year is in early fall, but the break does not last anywhere as long as in more northern states. In middle states northward to Massachusetts, I know from experience that bird feeders remain relatively inactive from about mid-August until late October. The same seems to hold true at feeders of about the same latitude farther west. It takes this long for the exodus of southbound migrants to be completed. At the same time, there is little replacement from the north in the way of juncos, white-throats, white-crowns, and others that will be spending the winter. These hardy birds wait until the chill winds of autumn before finally scurrying southward. It should be remembered that fall migration is conducted in a much more leisurely fashion than is seen in spring, when birds are hastening to reach nesting grounds.

### How it began

Food is only an indirect reason for the massive exodus that takes place each year in summer and fall. Ever since Aristotle, man has been trying to find a

suitable explanation for the disappearance of birds in fall and their reappear-
ance in the spring. As we have discovered, birds do not hibernate (except for
the poorwill) and do not journey to the moon. Instead, birds of many species
return year after year to the same wintering ground and with equal precision
come back to almost exactly the same nesting area. They do this regardless of
all but very drastic changes in food supply and climate.

As we now know, photoperiodism, in the form of changing daylength, is
the timetable that determines when birds will migrate. As days shorten through
late summer and into fall, birds respond to these differences in daylength by
initiating their migratory flights. The orchard oriole, to give an example of an
early migrant, begins leaving in mid-July and continues its departures into
September. In the spring, photoperiodism again comes into play; this time
longer daylength rather than shorter triggers the impulse to migrate. Rein-
forcing this instinct is the urge to mate and begin nesting. The motivation to
return is now so great for some species, like robins and bluebirds, that they
run the risk of overtaking winter and all its hazards. Birds that winter in the
tropics generally wait longer, but once they are back on our continent their
movements northward are comparatively rapid. In contrast to the fall, most
migration in spring will have been completed within a time span of only
about two months.

*Blackpoll warblers far out over the Atlantic on a*
*perilous 2,300-mile–nonstop flight to South America*

Daylight, not food, therefore, is the activating force behind the seasonal migration of most birds. At some dim period in the past, migration was forced upon birds by such slow, inexorable processes as subsidence, uplifting, shifting of continents, and advances and retreats of glaciers. Responding to these changes in the earth's surface, birds established migration routes that not always corresponded to the shortest distance between summer and winter homes. In North America many birds that nest in Alaska and western Canada, including the flicker, robin, yellow-rumped warbler, blackpoll, ovenbird, and dark-eyed junco, fly east in the fall before finally moving southward by way of the Mississippi or Atlantic Flyway. The same tortuous routes are again followed on the return trip in spring. As explained by Frederick C. Lincoln,* birds that take, what seem to us, unnecessarily long routes are ones that have gradually been expanding their ranges westward and have now reached western Canada and Alaska. The instinct to follow time-honored routes of the past is so deeply ingrained that the species in question are incapable of adapting to shorter migration routes. But indirectly food was responsible for the spectacular migrations that, since we are now in a warm cycle, seem less necessary. As glaciers receded or mountaintops became more habitable, birds moved into these uncrowded regions for the food and nesting sites they afforded. Any tendency to stay through the winter was cut short by the onset of heavy snows and severe cold; but even without these reminders, the urge was to return to the ancestral wintering grounds. Therefore the pattern was set ages ago—a descent from higher mountain ranges and a retreat from northern regions long before the arrival of winter. Many bird species today travel much farther than they have to in order to escape harsh conditions. They also often take longer, more circuitous routes than seem necessary. If we wonder why, we need to stop and consider the fact that they are responding to conditions that may have existed millions of years ago. The preconditioning, which began so long ago, isn't going to be changed overnight. Our feeding stations, therefore, are scarcely a factor in holding birds behind.

* Frederick C. Lincoln, *Migration of Birds* (Washington, D.C.: U.S. Dept. Fish and Wildlife Service, Circular 16, 1950).

It has been proved by radar in recent years that small migrant land birds leaving the coasts of Nova Scotia and New England in the fall take a course out over the Atlantic that, if maintained, would eventually bring them to the northwest coast of Africa. By taking advantage of a shift in wind direction, these bold flyers change their directional bearings somewhere far out over the Atlantic and veer toward the Antilles and coast of northern South America. The vireos, warblers, and other small birds that participate in these long flights always depart shortly after sunset and when the wind is favorable (behind them). There are other birds that carry out their migratory flights by day. Swifts, swallows, flickers, blue jays, many flycatchers, and hawks belong to the diurnal group of flyers. Shorebirds and waterfowl are about equally attuned to migrating by day or night. It is believed that nocturnal migration offers birds two advantages. They escape attacks by small-bird hawks, or accipiters, and, if lucky enough to be over land at daybreak, have the daylight hours free for feeding. Most of our small land birds do their migrating by night.

*Migrating Bohemian waxwings
strip trees of their fruit as they
move east and south in the fall.*

To prepare for the great adventure, birds for weeks feed heavily and put on layers of fat. Some of the small warblers I used to band at our fall mist-netting station on Nantucket were nearly twice their normal weight at this stage of their journey. This was particularly true of the blackpoll warbler, a bird that makes a nonstop, overwater flight of more than 2,300 miles lasting an average of eighty-six hours. The extra fat will serve as fuel as birds, departing from our coasts, tirelessly wing their way over the far reaches of the Atlantic.

### Wandering

Fall is also the season for nomadic wanderers. Leaving breeding grounds in Alaska and western Canada, flocks of Bohemian waxwings move southward, methodically stripping trees and bushes of fruits as they go. Somewhere in Canada the flocks part company, some moving eastward into Ontario and adjacent regions of our northern states, while others move southward down the backbone of the Rockies. These southward-moving flocks eventually fan out into towns and cities at lower elevations where supplies of ornamental fruits will see them through the winter. The debonair manner and handsome groomed appearance of these birds make them popular additions wherever they appear.

Much the same can be said of the cedar waxwing, a smaller edition of the Bohemian with a much wider range. In winter cedar waxwings can be found from coast to coast and as far south as Panama. Although the flocks slowly move southward in the fall, birds may spread out in any direction. Two cedar waxwings banded in California and recovered in Alabama provide an example of how far birds may stray from normal lanes of migration. Both waxwings are predictable in one respect. Their wandering is dictated by food; and when they come upon favorite fruits, they eat until they almost burst.

Other food-oriented migrations are also taking place at this season. Red-headed woodpeckers become so dependent upon acorns and beechnuts in fall and winter that they literally move with the nut harvest. If the nut harvest is plentiful in the north, the northern red-head population stays where it is through the winter. If the crop fails, which happens every few years, birds stream southward. When a mass exodus takes place there is no assurance that the birds will return in the spring. Redheads are true nomads that seem to come and go as they please. I have noticed that particularly favorable oak groves are seldom without these conspicuous woodpeckers so gaudy in their black, white, and red plumage. To keep from having to move so often, red-heads busily store acorns away in crevices when the harvest is good. The far west has its busybody counterpart in the acorn woodpecker. Food storing is such a passion with this bird that literally thousands of holes may be drilled into the trunks of large trees as storage repositories. Like its eastern cousin, acorn woodpeckers leave *en masse* when there is a crop failure.

Still other wanderers are to be found among the northern finches. Leaving their homes in the northern evergreen forest when cone and seed crop failures take place, the finches embark upon massive flights that overshadow anything undertaken by woodpeckers. The flights are spectacular both because of the numbers involved and the distances covered. Evening grosbeaks have been outperforming themselves in recent years by flying all the way to northern Florida and the Gulf states during some winters. Those of us who have feeding stations lying in the path of these hungry finches are apt to get the impression that the birds are motivated entirely by a craving for sunflower seeds. This is only partially

*Tennessee warbler in winter in Central America*

true, since the flocks subsist to a large extent upon a wide variety of natural plant foods.

Each of the northern finches has its own food specialties and feeding habits; therefore crop failures in the north rarely have an impact on all species. Many of the finches, as well as birds in other families like the red-breasted nuthatch, boreal chickadee, and gray jay, come south only if disastrous crop failures, affecting plants from pines to birches, take place. When this happens, we witness one of the rare invasion years which see an unbelievable variety of northern birds at feeding stations. Some of the rarely seen visitors go only as far as more northern states, while others appear almost anywhere within our borders. The average winter sees maybe two or three northerners at our feeders, as well as the ubiquitous American goldfinch and widely ranging purple finch.

In spite of their nomadic habits, the goldfinch and purple finch shouldn't be placed in the same category of "northerners" as pine and evening grosbeaks, pine siskins, crossbills, and redpolls. The first two nest in more intermediate latitudes and do not wait for crop failures to launch them forth in the fall. The American goldfinch even has the audacity to fly north from its breeding range during some fall and winter seasons. Canadians regard this bird as a

*Wintering Blackburnian warblers are one of the most common birds in the wooded highlands of Colombia.*

southern finch and look upon the purple finch as somewhat southern. How we classify birds depends a good deal upon where we live.

## Wrong directions

Contrary to popular belief, the impulse in the fall is not all directed toward flying south. Almost completely sedentary species, like the Carolina wren, summon up enough courage to inch northward if vacant territory lies in that direction. The red-bellied woodpecker, tufted titmouse, cardinal, and mockingbird, although generally regarded as permanent residents, keep pushing their ranges northward. The timing of the northward movement is early fall. Mockingbirds occasionally turn up in Nova Scotia in the fall, which is well north of the breeding range.

Ever so many small birds, as we birdbanders have discovered in our mist-netting operations (and later confirmed by radar), also move northward in the fall. Whether these birds fly north on their own or are carried by contrary winds is not known. In any event many of these vagrants reach small islands like Nantucket or appear elsewhere along the coast. Eventually most seem to become reoriented and join the main movement southward. But always a few, including stray yellow-breasted chats, remain in the north to face an uncertain future.

The cardinal, usually regarded as a staid "homebody," does its share of wandering. Besides a northward movement, probably involving only a relatively few individuals, cardinals also scatter out into nearby fields and woodlands in response to the common urge among birds in fall to fly about more than usual. These short journeys are not necessarily related to better-tasting or richer food supplies in the wild. Cardinals never seem to tire of the grain and sunflower at our feeders. Wanderlust may be the real reason. Occasional cardinals embark upon quite long journeys. A bird that traveled from Hartford, Connecticut, to State College in Pennsylvania was moving in a direction opposite to that of the seasonal bird migration. Banded in Hartford in December, the bird seems to have remained in the same place until taking flight for Pennsylvania in April.

Birds like chickadees and nuthatches seem to work off their migratory restlessness by wandering farther afield than usual. This is why we see so much less of them at feeders for a period in early fall. The movements of our resident chickadees and nuthatches, which may be in any direction, should not be confused with the previously mentioned "irruptions" that take place some years when food shortage or population pressure (or both) send residents of the northern forest streaming southward.

### The tropics at last

By far the greatest number of small land-bird migrants from North America take up winter residence in Central America and northern South America. A number stop off in the West Indies, while the blackpoll warbler and red-eyed vireo go all the way to the Amazonian forests of Brazil. Upon reaching their verdant winter homes, the new arrivals must learn about food, shelter, and water, and how to avoid enemies. Individuals that have spent the winter in the tropics before will quickly take up old ways. But the transition from north to tropics must be difficult for birds-of-the-year making their first migration southward. They learn by watching other birds and are assisted of course by instinct. Adults and young alike tend to join forces with mixed flocks of tropical birds. In spite of more intensive competition for food caused by greater numbers, there is little friction between residents and newcomers. When pressure for food and living space becomes too great for residents, some go to the lowlands where fewer migrants pass the winter; others stay where they are but often seek out less-used food. Instead of relying so much upon insects, which during the winter dry season may be in short supply, both residents and migrants now supplement their diets with nectar of flowers and tropical fruits.

Unfortunately, according to an article that appeared on August 12, 1980, in *The New York Times,* many of our migrant songbirds are beginning to decrease because of the destruction of mature forests in Central and South America. The forests are disappearing at a rate of 1 to 2 percent a year.

During visits in winter to Central America and the West Indies, I have been struck by the preponderance of migrants in comparison with local birds. This was not so true in the lowlands or more southern islands in the West Indies. In the highlands of Guatemala and Costa Rica, the North American warblers were sometimes the most conspicuous and numerous birds. In tree-shaded coffee plantations, Tennessee warblers often outnumbered all other birds. Flowering trees in city plazas were sometimes alive with colorful northern orioles and rose-breasted grosbeaks. Robert M. Chipley, writing in *The Living Bird* for 1976, reported that migrants made up about 50 percent of all birds in a disturbed oak forest in the highlands of Colombia. Blackburnian warblers accounted for about one-fourth of the winter bird population. That this warbler should be so abundant in its winter quarters may come as a surprise to those of us who feel lucky if able to catch a glimpse of this bird as it passes through in spring or fall. How many other bird species have we wrongly assumed to be rare or uncommon?

When I visited the well-known ornithologist Alexander F. Skutch at his home in the wilds of Costa Rica, I was astonished to find that the Tennessee warbler was the most common bird at his feeding station. With us the Tennessee, like the Blackburnian, is a rarely seen warbler and almost unknown at feeding stations.

A board attached to the trunk of a guava tree and never containing foods other than banana or plantain, the Skutch feeder attracted a surprisingly varied segment of the local bird population. Over a period of years, Dr. Skutch had recorded no less than twenty-six bird species at his modest feeder. Guests ranged from colorful resident honeycreepers, tanagers, and euphonias to occasional migrants from the north. Besides the Tennessees at the tray, there were fair numbers of wintering northern orioles and summer tanagers. The appearances of these birds had little effect upon relationships at the feeding shelf. Although the northern orioles squabbled among themselves, they were tolerant toward their tropical tablemates; and these birds in turn usually fed peacefully with each other and newcomers from the north. The summer tanagers came nervously and never stayed long. Nevertheless, their presence added a touch of color to an already colorful scene. They were the only all-red birds at the Skutch feeder.

Bird feeding is a popular pastime in some parts of the American tropics. Not only do individuals maintain feeding stations, as in the North, but many hotel proprietors have discovered that bird feeding is a tourist attraction. The most common location for a bird feeder is near the dining room where guests seated at their tables can watch the birds. The menu at the bird feeder consists largely of table scraps, fruit, and sugar in some form. Fats, seed, and grain are seldom used.

Thanks to bananaquits, colorful, impertinent little birds belonging to the honeycreeper family, sugar is a must at every West Indian bird feeder. Known for robbing sugarbowls and accepting sugar solutions at hummingbird feeders, bananaquits go a step farther and sometimes frequent barrooms for the sweetish liqueurs and other sweetish strong drink they can obtain from nearly empty glasses and corks of bottles. The birds become somewhat woozy at times and even lead other bird species down the same primrose path. But this may be giving a one-sided picture. Bananaquits obtain most of their food by visiting flowers and sampling fruit. Sugar is mostly a dessert.

At the Grafton Estate in Tobago, bananaquits, along with half a dozen other bird species, come in endless streams to patronize sugarbowls and sugar-water feeders. Only a little less popular with the gathering were ripe bananas fastened to a porch railing. The largest number of birds kept to the ground, where there were inducements in the form of birdbaths and plentiful supplies of chicken mash scattered about. Besides doves of four species, a native thrush, and blue-gray tanagers, a flock of about one hundred chachalacas was attracted by the chicken mash. Turkey-sized birds, brownish and with long tails, the chachalacas were as much at home in nearby trees as on the ground. From time to time a few would fly to the veranda to accept handouts from guests. The most colorful among this exciting assemblage were blue-crowned motmots, which freely flew to one's hand for bread or fruit. The motmot is not only gorgeously attired in olive green and dazzling shades of blue, but, a bizarre touch, the shafts of the two long, central tailfeathers are always bare for a space near the tip.

During their sojourn in the West Indies, many of our North American warblers are as bold about coming to bird feeders or helping themselves as the native bird species. On my first visit to Cuba, I was pleasantly surprised to find a male black-throated blue warbler sharing my dining-room table with me. It fed happily on bread crumbs and other small tidbits. Years later, at Lisa Salmon's famous bird-feeding station at Rocklands near Montego Bay in Jamaica, I was to see black-throated blue warblers sharing sugarwater and other foods with bananaquits.

Miss Salmon, a Jamaican citizen of Welsh descent, began feeding birds in the late 1930s and presently has a clientele that includes streamer-tailed hummingbirds, bananaquits, grassquits, and saffron finches, as well as wintering warblers and indigo buntings from the north. Moreover, doves of four species throng to her patio floor and nearby bird table to accept liberal allowances of birdseed and banana. No less than two thousand ground doves are believed to divide their time between the Lisa Salmon feeders and nearby countryside. Still other bird species, besides those already mentioned, find their way, along with tourists, to Miss Salmon's home and bird feeders tucked away in wooded hills overlooking the Caribbean. The visitor coming here often has the thrill of finding a streamer-tailed hummingbird on his finger sipping sugarwater from a hand-held vial.

Used to the limited way in which warblers respond to food offerings in the North, I was once again impressed by the varied appetites and frequent appearances of wintering warblers at the Lisa Salmon feeders. Black-throated blues divided their time between sugarwater, their favorite, and granulated sugar,

*Bananaquits in the Caribbean feeding at*
*a sugar bowl*

banana, or cheese. Cape May warblers were equally common and responded to the same foods. If anything, this inhabitant of the northern coniferous forest preferred fruit—both cultivated fruit made available at feeders and fruits obtainable on its own in the wild. Ovenbirds, looking like officials at an athletic contest, walked about the patio floor with an air of importance and from time to time picked up pieces of food. The tastes of this ground-loving warbler ran to cracked corn, millet, boiled rice, and banana. The preference for banana, which we have already seen in so many birds, even extended to wintering indigo buntings coming to the Lisa Salmon feeders.

Although winter visitors exhibited a wider range of food preferences than one would expect of the same species in the north, I was surprised to learn that sunflower went unrecognized and uneaten. Suet or fats, little used because of problems with ants, were taken only by the Jamaican woodpecker, the island's native species. On the other hand, cheese, a high-protein food, was extremely popular with nearly all visitors, both native birds and migrants. Whenever Miss Salmon wanted to invite a bird to feed from her hand, she offered cheese. Its

*The chachalaca is a common visitor to feeding stations on the island of Tobago.*

charm worked equally well with doves, warblers, and small finches. In spite of so many inviting foods, *water* was still the chief attraction, as it is everywhere in the West Indies.

As might be expected, such hospitality was inducement enough to keep many of Miss Salmon's visitors coming back a second or third year. Thanks to banding, she is able to keep tabs on many of her birds and is able to tell if they come back or not. When one thinks of the hazards of migration and the many dangers that birds face both on their breeding and wintering grounds, it is a wonder that there are any returns. Miss Salmon, nevertheless, has recorded quite a number. Mr. J. M. Harvey, playing host to birds at another Jamaican feeding station, recorded the presence of the same black-throated blue warbler winter after winter. The bird's loyalty seemed partly inspired by the ready availability of scrambled egg. The bird finally achieved a record of seven successive winters in Jamaica. Not bad for a bird whose summer home may have been somewhere in Ontario!

### Return north

One might expect that birds that spend the winter farthest from us would be the first to begin their migration northward. Not at all. With the one notable exception of the purple martin, that begins leaving Brazil in December, almost before our winter has begun, birds that go to the tropics stay there until the last minute. Like many who go to Florida for the winter, the tendency of migrants is to wait until all danger of snow and frost is past.

For first signs of movement in late winter, one should watch birds that live closer to home. In California, the most westward-ranging of our hummingbirds, the Allen's, begins its northward migration in January. In New England, crows, not bluebirds or robins, are the first spring migrants. Crows begin to arrive in mid-February. Scarcely harbingers of spring, they put in an appearance when winter is close to its worst. Even the skunk cabbage, the first of the spring wildflowers, hasn't sent its fetid shoots above the snow at this early date.

The presence of robins, so often regarded as a first sign of spring, is not a very reliable indicator. Although most robins travel all the way to the deep South, some do stay behind, and it is these birds that cause confusion. Newly arriving robins begin to appear in the North in early March. The eastern blue-bird falls into much the same category as the robin. A few stay rather far north, while others begin to return at about the same time as the early robins. At least this was true before the sharp decline in the bluebird population that has taken place over the last several decades. Now we are lucky if we see this bird at all in many parts of its once-wide range. Killdeer and woodcock also push north-ward at early dates. A few reach northern states by late February and early March.

The meaning of these early appearances is not clear. Some birds apparently respond earlier than others to lengthening daylight and move northward even though they may be ill prepared for wintry conditions. Getting back early may improve chances of obtaining mates and desirable nesting territory. But to return when snow is still on the ground seems to be carrying things too far.

Most birds, impatient though they be, wait until moderating conditions make travel northward less risky. Movements forward coincide with warm air

*Fair numbers of robins spend the winter in the North.*

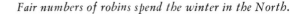

masses coming up from the South. When the wind swings around to the north
and the temperature falls, birds wait. Thus migration in spring progresses
through a series of rushes, each of which is followed by waits. Thanks to hollow
bones and air sacs sensitive to atmospheric pressure, birds are believed to be able
to detect weather changes as accurately as aneroid barometers. They become
nervous and agitated when the pressure begins to drop sharply. When migrating
birds, through their sensitivity, receive warning of an approaching blizzard or
snowstorm, they often have time to beat hasty retreats. That they are not always
successful in eluding returns of winter is seen in the way snowbound migrants
come flocking to our yards. The famished birds are grateful for anything at
all edible that we can give them.

By March small flocks of male red-wings, resplendent in their glossy black
plumage and red shoulder epaulets, are roving the countryside. Every few mo-
ments the birds burst forth into a joyful "o-ka-leee," which sounds like an
expression of pleasure at being back and alive after a long winter. It will be
another two to three weeks before the carefree males are joined by streaked,
buffy females whose one purpose is to get on with nest building and egg laying.

In contrast to red-wings newly arrived from the South are other red-wings
that have passed the winter quite far north. These survivors of the snow and
cold, along with grackles, starlings, and others that have stayed behind, seem
less joyful. They are still recovering from the hardships of winter and need a
few weeks of warmth and sunshine to revive their spirits. Much the same can be
said of the half-hardy mourning doves, catbirds, brown thrashers, orioles, and
towhees that have made it through the winter with the help of feeding stations. Will they stay more or less where they are or move northward along with
the general stream of migrants?

Besides birds that have spent the winter with us, our feeders now receive
hurrying flocks of juncos, fox sparrows, white-throats, and others that are passing
through on their way north. The flocks will stop by for a few days to feed, and
perhaps await favorable weather, before resuming their flights northward.
Chances are that none of these birds will have been in our yards before. Birds
are faithful to wintering and nesting grounds but not to exact locations along
their migration routes. The newcomers are quick to follow the example of long-

established patrons. They watch the other birds to see where they obtain food and water and go to shelter at night.

As March passes into April, established residents begin to feel the same restless urge that grips birds during fall migration. On springlike days, chickadees, along with the rest of the feeding-station company, take to nearby yards and woodlots. But there will be no repetition of early fall's scarcity. Far less natural food being available, birds are much more dependent upon feeding stations. Even on the finest days there will be early-morning and late-evening feeding periods. As soon as the temperature drops, or there is a threat of snow, birds are back again in normal numbers.

In contrast to the fall, there is much more overlapping between departures and arrivals. At the same feeding tray on a spring morning, I have seen indigo buntings and rose-breasted grosbeaks, fresh from the tropics, dining alongside evening grosbeaks and pine siskins. The cosmopolitan atmosphere that now pervades reminds one of the mixture of passengers at a large airport. Some have arrived from distant places and are waiting for connecting flights; others reaching the airport by bus or taxi are embarking on initial flights. While waiting for their respective flights, many of the passengers pass the time at the airport restaurant. If bad weather should set in, some of the flights may have to be canceled. Birds, too, eat and wait when bad weather sets in.

Finally the assembled company at our bird feeders in spring sorts itself out. In more southern states, the last of the winter visitors will have departed by mid-May. Farther north, evening grosbeaks sometimes linger into June. Through most of the winter, these voracious eaters will have limited their visits to morning hours. But as the departure time approaches, birds stay much later into the day and may even be seen feeding as we sit down to supper. These late sessions could be for extra fat needed to better sustain them on their journey north. Goldfinches and pine siskins, which keep no special feeding hours, leave so suddenly that we feel affronted. Present in normal numbers one day, they are gone the next. These impromptu departures are characteristic of most smaller finches. Other of our visitors seem reluctant to leave and give the appearance of postponing their departures as long as possible. Writing of the fall departure of a flock of chipping sparrows in a 1923 issue of *The Auk*, Charles L. Whittle tells how the birds apparently came back for a farewell visit. The entire flock with their progeny disappeared in late August. Then, on September 5, the flock was back for "a last glimpse before leaving." Aaron C. Bagg* takes much the same view of late visits by bluebirds. He says they come back in October "as if to say goodbye to their homes."

These somewhat sentimental interpretations may not be too farfetched. Birds do exhibit very strong attachments to both breeding grounds and winter territory. Departures must come as a jolt. Haven't we all seen examples of birds that turn up again after we thought they had left? The interpretation we usually give is that weather had forced a return. Could it be that in some cases birds do pay a final farewell?

### The great mystery

Our yard, however, small and hidden away it may be, is the target of birds during the migration seasons. Some stop off during spring migration to stay long enough to nest and raise families, others come back each fall to spend the winter and avail themselves of the food and shelter we offer. Our yard will play host to hurrying migrants that pause long enough to feed and rest, and also to the occasional stray far off course whose presence will lend spice to our bird watching.

Ability to find our yard is no less a mystery than ability to find a small island in the Caribbean or a clump of sedges that is an Arctic nest site. During the day, migrating birds seem strongly influenced by topographical features. They follow coastlines and rivers but avoid flying over broad bodies of water. On reaching the tip of a peninsula, diurnal migrants often turn back and retrace their course. This sequence of events is frequently seen at Point Pelee in Ontario in the fall. Migrants reaching the tip of the point turn back rather than strike out over Lake Erie. Even at night migrating birds sometimes move in an opposite direction to the one that will take them toward their destinations. Reverse

* Aaron C. Bagg and Samuel A. Eliot, Jr., *Birds of the Connecticut Valley in Massachusetts* (Northampton, Mass.: Hampshire Bookshop, 1937).

migration is a not uncommon phenomenon among migrants. There are also times when birds are blown off course.

It is well known that some birds have an incredible ability to find their way back after being released hundreds or even thousands of miles from their nesting sites. A manx shearwater from Wales in Britain was taken to Boston and released. The bird was back in twelve days, having accomplished a flight of three thousand miles. Equally amazing is the ability of birds to set out for a distant target and arrive there without the benefit of our navigational instruments. Murres, seabirds belonging to the group known as alcids, were observed flying unerringly through dense fog off the coast of Alaska toward their nesting colonies many miles away.

Many theories have been advanced to account for the way birds are able to reach their goals, day or night, fair weather or foul. No one theory seems to account for the extraordinary navigational abilities shown by birds under a variety of conditions. That they are aided by bearings they obtain from the moon and stars at night and the sun in the daytime seems highly probable. Forces in the universe, like the earth's magnetic field and gravitational pull, according to latest theories, may also help birds find their way.

For a good summary of the various theories, I suggest that the reader consult John K. Terres's encyclopedia.* In spite of all the progress that has been made in the study of bird migration, researchers, according to Terres, freely admit that they still have far to go in learning the secrets. A bird may follow more than one cue in finding its way to its destination and may even prefer one cue or aid over another.

Whatever the gift or gifts birds may have, their extraordinary abilities are completely beyond anything the human species possesses. We should feel a certain amount of awe when birds appear in our yards each spring and fall with such uncanny precision.

* John K. Terres, *The Audubon Society Encyclopedia of North American Birds* (New York: Alfred A. Knopf, 1980), pp. 606–8.

# Food | 2

The kind of food they eat and the way they eat it tell us a lot about both birds and people. If we are already prejudiced against a bird species, say, the starling, and observe it eating like a glutton, this only helps confirm our poor impression. Of course, in judging people, we are advised not to go too much by outward appearances. The same should apply equally well to birds. After all, manners are a human invention. Birds and other animals obtain their food the best way they can. If some species are gentle and retiring in the way they eat, this is because this method suits them best. We approve of the cedar waxwing's gentle manners and the way it shares food with its fellows. An "after you, Alphonse" deference is sometimes seen when birds pass food from bill to bill; this may be a rite related to courtship. In any event, waxwings have little need to fight, since the flocks, outside the nesting season, are nomadic, following their food supply.

In contrast, a mockingbird, dependent upon a limited number of berry-laden shrubs to sustain it through the winter, can hardly afford to be welcoming. It must protect its supply from other fruit-eating birds, including mock-ingbirds. If, as now and then happens, a mockingbird becomes overly zealous and begins to deny other birds access to the feeding station, we find ourselves with one of those difficult problems that now and then crop up when we under-take our philanthropic venture into helping birds by feeding them. There are solutions, as I have pointed out in my *Complete Guide to Bird Feeding*. But most of the time, why not forget about being arbitrators and enjoy birds for what they are—fascinating forms of life that do a pretty good job of looking out for their needs without the complicated codes that govern human behavior?

*Amounts eaten*

"Birdlike appetite" is an expression little used these days. Perhaps this is because there are so many people with feeding stations who know only too well what bird appetites are like. Birds eat with an intensity that is sometimes frightening. It took nine tons of sunflowers one winter to keep up with bird appetites at State College, Pennsylvania. For a while, hummingbirds at sugarwater feeders near Zion National Park in Utah were consuming five gallons of solution a day. And to mention the inroads that one bird can make, a scrub jay at a California feeding station was observed making off with a hundred sunflower seeds in twenty-five minutes.

But do birds for their size really eat so much more than other warm-blooded animals? Judging by the performance of small mammals at feeding stations, I think most of us would prefer the appetites of birds to those of squirrels. Even

*Chipmunk returning to its burrow with a full load*

the chipmunks that fill their cheek pouches with seeds and scamper away are an economic factor to be reckoned with. One feeding-station operator ruefully noted that a pair of chipmunks carried off a hundred pounds of wild birdseed during a single fall season. The blue jay, so addicted at times to storing food, can hardly compete with this record. So perhaps we shouldn't single out birds as being any more gluttonous than most animals, including ourselves.

Birds owe their large appetites partly to rapid digestion. Experiments reported upon by James Stevenson in a 1933 issue of *The Wilson Bulletin* give approximately one and a half hours as the time required for food to pass through the digestive systems of a number of species (mostly sparrows). But Daniel E. Owen, writing in an early issue of *The Auk,* reported that it took only half an hour for blueberries to appear in the droppings of a captive hermit thrush. It is likely that fruits and berries pass as quickly as this through the digestive tracts of our two species of waxwings. The birds stop gorging themselves only long enough to stay perched in a semicomatose condition for twenty or thirty minutes and then back they go to the feast again.

As everyone with a feeding station knows, birds begin eating much more heavily whenever there is a conspicuous drop in temperature. This is clearly seen in careful attendance records kept by Charles F. Leck* of Princeton, New Jersey. He noted a dramatic increase in number of visits by birds to his feeding station with every 10 to 20 degrees drop in temperature. For example, he counted six times as many visits per day by house finches and other birds when the temperature had fallen from an average of 40 to 60 degrees to 20 to 30 degrees F. During snowstorms or periods of snow cover there was an even more dramatic increase in attendance.

Many of us have the impression that larger birds are the greatest freeloaders. This is partly the fault of birds like jays, grosbeaks, and blackbirds, and not altogether true. We are apt to take more notice of the jay's poor manners because they are so obvious. Usually arriving with a flourish, jays come three, four, or more at a time, load up on food, and then fly off. A jay holds some food in its beak as it flies away, but usually much more is tucked in an enlargement

* Charles F. Leck, "Temperature and Snowfall Effects on Feeding Station Activity," *Bird-Banding* 49 (3): 283–4.

of the throat known as the craw or gullet. I had no idea how much food a blue jay holds in this enlargement until I got a bird, freshly out of my banding trap, to cough up all it held. The surprising total was sixty-six items, consisting mostly of wheat kernels as well as a few pieces of corn. In Florida I noticed that blue jays harvesting acorns in a grove of oak trees would deposit two acorns in the gullet and hold a third in the beak as they flew off to hide the food for future needs. A scrub jay in California was seen to carry twelve sunflower seeds at a time, always one or two of them in the beak. In contrast chickadees, which use only the beak for holding food, carry away only one, or, at the most, two sunflower seeds at a time.

Not a bird to carry away or hide food, the evening grosbeak does all its eating in full view. The sunflower seeds disappear so quickly that we can almost hear the ring of the cash register. One observer, taking stock of the situation at his feeder, noted that a single evening grosbeak consumed ninety-six sunflower seeds in less than five minutes. But, unlike blue jays, evening grosbeaks are with us irregularly only through the winter and sometimes into June; moreover, except toward the end of their stay, they rarely pay afternoon visits.

Although not exactly a modest eater, the red-winged blackbird is perfectly content with scratch feed and other lesser fare. When banding red-wings in Florida, I found that occasionally a bird in the excitement of being herded out of a trap would inhale a millet seed. In a few seconds the bird would die of

*In spite of their voracious appetites, evening grosbeaks are welcome visitors at most feeding stations.*

asphyxiation. Other banders, like myself, have had this happen with red-wings and cowbirds. These rare accidents are probably not a result of overeating. Even so, a red-wing that died in one of my traps through inhaling a millet seed had taken 511 other millet seeds in addition to the fatal one.

The smaller birds do not do so badly either when it comes to consuming food. They eat more in comparison to their size than larger birds, and spend much more time searching for food. After cold weather sets in, small birds like kinglets, chickadees, nuthatches, and brown creepers spend virtually the entire daylight period in a never-ending search for food. They eat on the run, or, more correctly, on the wing, often looking for the next morsel while still downing the scanty substance that came from the last tiny eggs or scale insects. With the shorter daylight hours of winter, small birds are often hard put to find enough food to maintain the vigorous pace they must set for themselves. That is good reason why the winter feeding station is so popular with birds.

As with jays and magpies, a number of other small birds put food away for hard times. Woodpeckers, particularly the acorn species, red-headed, and red-bellied, are the greatest hoarders of all. But occasionally chickadees or nuthatches will take it upon themselves to transfer as much of the feeding station as they can to nearby hiding places. Filling their bills with suet, sunflower seeds, and other foods, they embark upon a feverish program that often goes unnoticed or ignored. People are much more sympathetic with small birds and overlook their foibles.

A white-breasted nuthatch at my Virginia feeder used to spend much of the day carrying off small pieces of suet and hiding them carelessly in bark crevices of nearby trees. During a half-hour watch, I saw this bird remove no less than thirty-eight pieces of suet. Some of the pieces were tucked into the bark of a tree trunk only a few feet away. Normally food-storing birds are more careful than this and take pains to conceal their stores. They know from experience that there are many watchful eyes taking in their every move. Even the unobtrusive brown creeper pilfers the hastily made caches of the white-breasted nuthatch, as do chickadees and blue jays. The blue jay, in turn, may have its stores ransacked by crows, as noted by a birdbander in Cleveland, Ohio, or by gray squirrels, as I have noted in my yard in Maryland. Jays coming to my yard, instead of following their usual procedure of hiding food under leaves or pressing it into soft ground, were on to a new trick—tucking pecan nuts from a nearby tree and odd scraps into the dense evergreen foliage of boxwood (*Buxus sempervirens*) hedges. This ruse was no more successful than others in foiling pilferers. Sharp-eyed gray squirrels quickly caught on and began stealing the food almost as soon as it was deposited. A red-headed woodpecker, spending the winter in New Hampshire, had its stores of grain and suet taken by a hairy woodpecker. So goes the never-ending cycle of storing and robbery in which the victimized party never quite catches on to what is happening.

There is always the temptation to eat the food before some other bird or a squirrel steals it. This was the case with chickadees that were hiding suet in a woodpile in the morning and coming back in the afternoon to eat it. According to Susan Smith,* Carolina chickadees, when confronted with the superabundance of a new feeding station, immediately begin to store food; so does a

* Susan Smith, "Communication and Other Social Behavior in *Parus carolinensis*" (Cambridge, Mass.: Nuttall Ornithological Club, 1972).

*Red-headed woodpeckers store acorns in fence posts and seal them in with bits of plant debris.*

chickadee that for the first time begins visiting an old feeding station. In time the bird relaxes and, as it were, puts more confidence in us and our resolve never to let feeders stay empty.

A white-breasted nuthatch at a neighbor's feeder, unlike the one at mine, always took the precaution of covering over its stores with pieces of bark or lichen. As I watched this bird one day, it carefully tucked a sunflower seed in the bark crevice of an old oak tree trunk; then it dropped to the ground and picked up a piece of bark. Returning to the cache, it placed the bark over the seed, and, as a final precaution, hammered upon the bark lid until it was firmly in place. I had the feeling that with all these precautions not even the nuthatch itself would be able to find its store again. But, as with jays, woodpeckers, and squirrels, the aim seems to be to make enough stores so that at least some of them will be found later on.

In Florida, I saw red-headed woodpeckers storing acorns in crevices in fence posts and using almost exactly the same technique as the white-breasted nuthatch to seal them in. The only difference was that the woodpeckers were covering their supplies with small sticks instead of using bark or lichen. I suppose, whether nuthatch or woodpecker, the bird uses the material that happens to be most handy. The acorn woodpecker in California and other parts of the West uses still another technique. True to its name, it spends a good part of the year gathering and storing acorns. These are hammered into holes in tree trunks, fence posts, and even houses, where the owners are reasonably sympathetic. Each hole is just large enough to contain the species of oak acorn that the birds happen to be storing. The birds may come back weeks or months later to retrieve their stores.

Gallinaceous birds, raptors, parrots, doves, and others have a distendable pouch or enlarged gullet known as the crop. After a mourning dove, for example, has filled its crop with food, it must wait for some of this food to reach the rest of the alimentary tract and finally the stomach. When it can choke down no more food, the mourning dove that has been feeding at a feeding station will fly off to roost in a tree or a sunny spot on the ground. Here with the rest of the flock it will sit quietly and perhaps do some preening while the digestive processes do their work. Almost no digestion will take place in the crop, which is primarily a storage bin. Birds with crops have the advantage of not having to eat so often, and they have a second advantage in being able to carry their emergency rations with them. The crop normally holds four or five times the volume that the stomach does. This will be clear to anyone who has cleaned a chicken that has eaten its fill.

A ground dove that met with an accident after eating at my Florida feeding station had 697 seeds and pieces of grain in its stomach and crop, which is a lot of food for such a small bird. The much larger, more northerly ranging ruffed grouse can carry quite a supply in its crop. Figures supplied by Gardiner Bump and his co-workers* show that the ruffed grouse can eat enough poison ivy berries at a sitting to keep many of us itching for weeks or months. A bird killed in Arkansas had eaten no less than 3,000 berries of this poisonous plant. Two ruffed grouse taken in the Northeast also had hearty appetites—one had eaten 1,400 buds of wild cherry while the other had taken fifty strawberries that contained between them no less than 4,350 seeds. However, for ability to stuff its crop full of very small items, the prize, so far as I know, goes to a ring-necked pheasant in Washington that had eaten 8,000 seeds of chickweed and a dandelion head. Extra stores, such as these, can come in handy when bad weather sets in. But according to John Terres, a mallard shot in Louisiana contained over 75,000 food items in its stomach and another mallard from Louisiana had eaten 102,400 seeds of primrose willow (*Ludwigia* sp.).

Stocking up on food at the approach of a winter blizzard in Pennsylvania, a flock of domestic turkeys on an outdoor range took the same kind of precautions that their wild cousins would have under similar circumstances. They ate more than usual and then burrowed under the snow. Here they stayed until the storm was over. When they emerged four days later, the relieved turkey farmer found his charges none the worse for their experience. The birds had lived on stored fat and the food held in reserve in their capacious crops.

* Gardiner Bump, Robert W. Darrow, Frank C. Edminster, and Walter F. Crissey, *The Ruffed Grouse: Life History, Propagation, and Management* (Albany, N.Y.: New York State Conservation Department, 1947).

Birds, like ourselves, are guided to a large degree by color when it comes to food
selection. The brightest colors are usually those that are most noticed by birds
and most appealing to their appetites. To be sure, birds have to learn to avoid
some brightly colored foods. Ladybird beetles or monarch butterflies, masquer-
ading in bright colors, need to be avoided because of their bad taste. Once a
bird has had an unpleasant experience or two with a brightly colored insect,
it tends to avoid all similarly colored insects—an advantage that the viceroy
butterfly has seized upon during the course of its evolution by mimicking the
ill-tasting monarch.

Red, poorly represented at the bird feeder, is almost certainly the most
important advertising color in the plant kingdom wherever the services of birds
are needed. This is *the* color that more than any other brings hummingbirds to
flowers and also hummingbird feeders. A. L. Pickens,* who has made a lifelong
study of the flower preferences of hummingbirds, calls red the undoubted favorite, with crimson tints preferred over scarlet. Without taking white into
consideration, he stated that violet was second choice, orange third, blue fourth,
yellow fifth, and green last. In another study he reported that white flowers

* A. L. Pickens, "The Eighth Bird and Nectar Census," *Chat* 32(1):5–6.

*Monarch butterflies and ladybird beetles*
*are brightly colored and bad tasting.*

were second only to red ones in attractiveness to hummingbirds. He makes the point that white, like black, is not a color in the strictest sense of the word.

Red appears in the ripe fruits and berries of plants that need the assistance of birds as an aid to dissemination. Birds only too obligingly eat the red fruits and later void or cough up hard pits or seeds. Experiments by S. Davis and colleagues, reported in a 1973 issue of *The Condor,* showed that sunflower seeds dyed red were even more popular at the feeder than natural undyed sunflower, while sunflower dyed yellow, green, or blue were less well received. Birds coming to the seeds in this experiment were plain titmice, western cousins of the well-known tufted titmouse.

White foods, in contrast to red, are much more widely used in bird feeding. On the whole, they are so quickly recognized and downed that we may be safe in thinking that whiteness has a special meaning for birds. Some of the most tempting bird foods in nature are white ants and white grubs. Birds of prey have a keen eye for any hapless albino or other white or partly white animal that is within their capacity. White is so conspicuous and so vulnerable that few animals, unless they are quite large or live in cold, snow-covered regions of the earth, survive long when dressed in this garb. Seabirds and some waders that have the sky and water as a background are exceptions.

*The white fruits of white mulberry are eagerly taken by birds.*

The plant kingdom produces few white fruits or berries, and many of these
are poisonous. This is true of mistletoe, poison ivy, and poison sumac. All three
are popular with birds and downed without ill effect. The snowberries, so often
planted for ornament, are eagerly taken by quail, pheasants, and other gallinaceous birds, but not so eagerly by songbirds. White-fruited mulberries and
dogwood berries vie in popularity with red-fruited ones. Charlotte Green, a
writer on southern birds and plants, says white mulberry is even more popular
with birds than red mulberry. White, as we have already seen, has been reported second only to red in floral colors attractive to hummingbirds.

Recollections of feasting in the wild could very well play a part in the
quick response that birds give to white foods at feeding stations. They are not
disappointed when they take our white bakery products and white suet. The
quickest way to get birds coming to a new feeding station is to offer them
conspicuous white foods. In England, titmice were offered foods that had been
dyed red, green, and violet with vegetable dyes or left white, if this was their
natural color. According to John A. G. Barnes, in his book *The Titmice of the
British Isles,** birds overwhelmingly chose the white foods.

White also looms importantly in nesting material. The tree swallow, if it
has access to chicken feathers, almost always takes white ones to line its nest.
Northern orioles go out of their way to use white string or yarn in constructing
their finely woven nests. On the late date of November 24, I saw house sparrows
and starlings near my Maryland home picking up white chicken feathers. The
house sparrows would roll the feathers around in their bills and then drop them,
while starlings, more purposefully, would fly off with the feathers. The feather
collecting was one of those examples of revival of the nesting instinct so often
seen in birds in late fall. At this time of the year, birds often go through all the
motions of nesting again, except for egg laying. It is not exceptional, however,
for mourning doves to still be nesting in October, while house sparrows, prolific birds that they are, are known to conduct nesting activity in every month
of the year. Although not late nesters, starlings have a habit during fall and
winter of looking over prospective nesting sites. I once watched a pair minutely
inspect a cavity in a maple tree in late January.

* John A. G. Barnes, *The Titmice of the British Isles* (London: David & Charles, 1975).

More in keeping with the season was a robin in late March that I saw picking up a piece of white tissue paper and wedging it into a crotch in a maple tree. Jean Bancroft of Winnipeg, Manitoba, has experimented with placing variously colored nesting materials for birds. She writes me that most birds, when nest building, can't resist flying off with white strips of Kleenex in their bills. She adds that white string and white cotton fluff from a clothes dryer are equally popular with birds that are engaged in nest building.

Next to white, the color that is seen most often at the feeding station is yellow. We see yellow in corn, cornbread, cornmeal, golden millet, and such occasional offerings as halved orange. The only food that prompted wintering bluebirds to come to a feeding station in the New York City area was yellow layer cake that had been crumbled. Similarly, northern orioles wintering at Wilmington, Delaware, responded only when offered yellow raisins.

In the wild, yellow foods receive a mixed reception. A European ornithologist, F. Turcek,[*] noted that colors about the center of the spectrum—orange, yellow, and green—are least attractive to birds. Of numerous species of woody plants in Europe offering fruits taken by birds, only seven had yellow fruits and two orange fruits. Other writers have commented on the fact that when birds have a choice of red- or yellow-fruited plants, they nearly always take the red fruits in preference to yellow ones. This has been noted in pyracantha hollies, cherries, mountain ashes, and other plants. In experiments aimed at finding a color that would keep birds from taking poison baits, yellow was next to green in effectiveness. As we have seen, hummingbirds do not respond well to yellow flowers; yet, in spite of the poor reception that yellow usually gets, there is a conspicuous exception.

Ever since the time of Charles Darwin, the British have been observing a distressing preference by house sparrows for yellow crocus blossoms. The birds single out the yellow blossoms to eat or tear apart while leaving those of other colors untouched. This perverse ravaging does not end with the crocus. Sometimes along with starlings, the sparrows go after other yellow flowers, including primroses, primulas, lesser celandine, dandelion, forsythia, and evening primrose. On our side of the Atlantic, a number of birds, including house sparrows,

---

* F. Turcek, "Color Preference in Fruit- and Seed-Eating Birds," *Proc. International Orni. Congr.* 13 (1963):285–92.

have a liking for the early buds and blossoms of forsythia. In Florida, I saw a
house sparrow making off with the yellow petals of puncture-weed (*Tribulus cistoides*), a troublesome weed, although a pretty one.

It would be interesting if only yellow flowers received this attention. Such attachment to a color might suggest that yellow flowers had something in them that birds needed. Unfortunately for this theory, birds do take flowers of other colors, and even the British house sparrows have been caught eating or tearing apart crocuses of other colors. To add to this already confusing picture, a pet crow in New Hampshire would tear to shreds purple crocus blossoms and leave those of other colors! The owner thought the bird disliked purple.

For the most part, birds eat only grudgingly the brown foods we offer at feeding stations; nevertheless they do quite well when it comes to all forms of the peanut and nutmeats. Sorghum, browntop millet, oats, and wheat are less favored, while birds have to be taught to eat doughnuts. Once a doughnut is broken and crumbled, thus exposing the more tempting interior, birds eagerly take to this food.

A large share of the seeds in the plant kingdom are hidden in brown envelopes. These range from the hard-shelled nuts to fragile grass seeds. However, the brown-coated harvest is so inconspicuous, and, in many instances, so hard to obtain that only a few groups of birds know how to exploit it. This is not an accident of nature. The plants in question have other means of dispersal and can do without birds. Although jays help the spread of oaks and nut trees by burying part of the harvest, most brown-coated seeds are destroyed when they are eaten by birds. For this reason, plants with more fragile seeds tend to hide their harvest under shades of brown, a ruse, however, that is not overly successful in thwarting most seed-eating birds.

Black seeds are much more conspicuous, and therefore black is effectively employed by plants in gaining the services of birds. Turcek lists a few more European bird species feeding on black fruits than red ones. We have our blackberries, elderberries, grapes, hackberries, and many others that may appeal to birds partly because black is such a popular color. Southward in the West Indies black seems dominant in plants that depend on birds for their transport. I noticed this on a visit to the Bahamas, where much of the flora owes its presence to birds.

Black by itself might not be conspicuous enough to capture the attention of birds. But nearly always the black is reinforced by a lustrous sheen that makes the seeds or fruits stand out more clearly. In many plants, the addition of red makes the feast even more visible. The fruits of Siebold viburnum, for example, are red before they turn black; moreover, the stems which hold the fruit are a bright red. Another plant that makes good use of black and red is pokeweed. Its berries, clinging to bright red stems, are a lustrous black when ripe; moreover, the green stalks and branches of the plant become a reddish-purple about the time the fruits begin to mature. Birds can hardly fail to take notice of such a vivid combination! They respond by flocking to the autumn-ripening fruits, which are somewhat toxic to people but perfectly safe for birds.

Until thistle (niger) caught on with those who feed birds, there were no popular, commercially available black foods to use in bird feeding. The small hanging thistle feeders with finches clinging to them and doves feeding on fallen seeds below are now a part of the bird-feeding scene everywhere. Less well-known is rape, a small black seed that is much less popular with birds but which attracts some of the same birds that thistle does. Black shows up again in all-black sunflower seeds. Experiments show that the black is just as popular with birds as conventional black-and-white-striped sunflower seed.

Blue and purple are all but absent at the feeder. These colors show up in nature in the form of flower blossoms and a number of fruits and berries. Grapes, always popular with birds, come in bluish-purple hues, as well as black, and it would be hard to find more tempting bird fruits than the blue ones of red cedar, blueberry, Asiatic sweetleaf, fringetree, and sassafras. It is somewhat out of place to mention the fact that the satin bowerbird in Australia uses blue flowers and other blue objects exclusively to decorate its bowers. But the bower-birds, like most Australian wildlife, have unexpected habits. The favorite color among bowerbirds generally is green!

Knowledge of how birds react to color has a practical application when it comes to choosing a proper color to use on birdhouses. I always avoided red, thinking it might repel potential customers. But Robert A. McCabe, writing in a 1961 issue of *The Condor,* reports that house wrens, when given a choice of red, yellow, blue, white, and green nesting boxes, preferred the reds and the greens. White houses were least used. McCabe, who had conducted his experiments over a period of eleven years, concluded that there was no clear-cut pattern of reaction to color by birds.

This would seem to be a sensible conclusion in light of the varied reactions we have seen by birds to such colors as green, red, and yellow. Under some circumstances a color invites, under others it repels. The red that is so inviting on a fruiting tree or the outside of a birdhouse may repel when it is worn by a beetle or butterfly. Birds, of course, are better aware of these distinctions than we are.

### Hidden food

It would seem that birds, or at least some birds, do not need color clues or good visibility to lead them to their food. Many birds are aware of completely hidden sources of food, and others need only a fleeting glimpse to tell them that a meal is at hand. We see this sometimes when our food offerings at the feeding station have been covered by snow. When an early snowstorm buried the food at my Moose Hill bird feeders, juncos burrowed through to birdseed on the ground

*Pokeweed, with its juicy fruits and bright coloring, is irresistible to fruit-eating birds.*

below a feeding tray. The birds did not dig but pushed their way through the soft snow.

Gray partridges and a ring-necked pheasant had no trouble digging through several inches of snow to a compartment in an experimental feeder for game birds in Wisconsin that held their favorite grain, which was corn. As reported in a 1937 *Journal of Wildlife Management,* these birds, together with prairie chickens and bobwhite quail, were coming to a test feeder with trays containing wheat, buckwheat, milo, scratch feed, and corn. The positions of the trays were frequently shifted so that the birds wouldn't select their food on the basis of position. That the corn-loving birds knew exactly where the corn was under newly fallen snow brings up still another mystery. How do birds sometimes unerringly locate seeds that have been freshly planted in a garden?

A California gardener, Frank A. Leach, reporting in a 1927 issue of *The Condor,* wondered what had been taking peas he had recently planted. Deciding that the culprits might have been brown towhees living in his yard, he kept a careful watch after making his second planting. Sure enough, the towhees were to blame! The birds returned, taking every single pea he had planted. The gardener had taken steps to carefully smooth over the ground after completing his plantings. Even so, the birds knew exactly where the peas were.

Clark's nutcracker, a crowlike bird of our western mountains, has the ability to dig unerringly through deep snow to a source of food. Victor H. Cahalane, as quoted in Bent's *Life Histories of North American Birds,** tells of a Clark's nutcracker that dug through eight inches of hard-packed snow to reach the cone of a Douglas fir tree. There was nothing at the surface of the snow to give the bird a clue. Perhaps the bird had seen the cone prior to the snowfall and knew where it lay in relation to a rock, tree, or some other landmark. In much the same way, the European nutcracker, a close relative, spends the winter digging through the snow to its carefully buried stores, which consist largely of hazelnuts. These nutcrackers have been reported to dig through as much as one and a half feet of snow to reach their caches!

Woodpeckers also show uncanny ability in finding unseen food. Species,

---

* A. C. Bent, *Life Histories of North American Jays, Crows, and Titmice* (Washington, D.C.: U. S. National Museum Bull. 191, 1946).

like the pileated, which obtain a large share of their food deep within the trunks
and branches of trees seem to depend to a large degree upon hearing in locating
their prey. The pileated woodpecker characteristically taps and listens a number
of times before starting one of its spectacular excavations. Always these lead
directly to a carpenter ant colony or other hidden insect life. The initial tapping
may serve to stir ants or other insects into moving about and giving their
position away; the woodpecker may also, by its tapping, be able to sound out
corridors where insects have tunneled through the wood.

The American robin, running a short distance, stopping, cocking its head,
and then perhaps snatching a worm from its hole, also seems to be using auditory
sense to locate prey. But Frank Heppner in a 1965 issue of *The Condor* reports
experimental evidence showing that robins locate their prey entirely by vision.
The bird cocks its head in order to look for any small portion of a worm that
might be visible near the surface. Worms are most apt to be on or close to the
surface in wet weather; they also tend to be close to the surface early in the
morning or in late afternoon. Robins are aware of this, and time their hunting
activities accordingly.

*Deep snow does not deter Clark's nutcracker*
*from reaching buried stores.*

The way in which birds are sometimes able to find hidden food suggests that they may have a sense of perception we are not even aware of and which is absent in the human species. We are able to find our way around in dim light or find certain objects by utilizing touch, smell, hearing, or vision. Birds are poorly equipped in regard to the first two of these senses but, for the most part, extremely proficient when it comes to hearing and vision. Some birds have sensory nerve endings in the bill or feet, which can be used to pick up vibrations made by underground forms of life. These nerve endings, however, could hardly tell birds where seeds had been planted or where stores of food lay under the snow. Sense of smell is very poorly developed in most birds. Exceptions to this rule are the turkey vulture, which locates food both by sight and smell, many petrels, and the kiwi, a flightless, nocturnal bird, living in New Zealand, that is said to locate worms and grubs largely through sense of smell.

John A. G. Barnes tells how titmice were unable to discover strong-smelling

*Pileated woodpecker sounding out a tree trunk for hidden insect life*

cheese placed under a loose piece of cloth. Cheese is one of the most popular foods among birds generally at British feeding stations. By the same token, Barnes tells us, sense of smell did not stop birds from eating foods that had been doctored with strong-smelling substances, including garlic, paraffin, lavender water, and vinegar. Taste, closely allied to sense of smell, did not stop the birds either. Apparently only extremes of taste are detected by birds. The few taste buds that birds are equipped with lie in the rear parts of the mouth; they assist birds in tasting some foods but not others. As we have already seen in titmice, birds may eat foods that are bitter or highly astringent. Either their taste buds do not pick up the bitter flavor, or the bitterness is not distasteful to them. The same reaction to bitter foods seems to prevail throughout most of the bird world, with only a few dissenters, including chickens and pigeons. According to experiments reported upon by John K. Terres, chickens and pigeons refused a number of bitter foods and were thought to have a well-developed sense of taste.

Certainly many of our feeding-station visitors show discrimination in the way they choose one food over another and sometimes reject a food completely. Like many of us, birds are suspicious of foods they have never seen before. A new food at the bird feeder may go untouched for days or even weeks. Whether taste plays a role in the selection of foods by birds at a feeder is debatable. Other factors, including size, shape, texture, and color of the food, may be equally important. While it is difficult to gauge the role that taste plays in choice of food by birds, it seems safe to say that birds generally respond well to sweetness, and, on the whole, like the same foods we do.

Hearing, as we have seen, is an important aid to woodpeckers in their search for hidden food. This sense appears to be even more highly developed in owls. On the darkest nights owls can capture their prey by hearing the slightest rustling sounds on the ground below. According to Lewis Wayne Walker,* a barn owl confined to a completely darkened shed was able to capture mice entirely through sense of hearing. But the presence of dry leaves was necessary for noise effects. The experiment explained why owls are less successful in capturing prey in wet weather. They need dry leaves if they are to hear their prey.

---

* Lewis Wayne Walker, *The Book of Owls* (New York: Alfred A. Knopf, 1974).

Vision, coupled with good memory, helps explain some of the more difficult feats performed by birds in finding hidden food. Memory alone might account for the ability of nutcrackers to dig through deep snow to uncover a hidden source of food. Birds have a keen sense of location. They return the following year to the exact site of a birdhouse or feeding station even though neither is in place. Even if a sugarwater vial is removed, hummingbirds will continue to visit the site as they make the rounds of the yard. But we are still faced with the problem of how the brown towhees could so unerringly locate buried peas that they themselves had never seen before.

### Mistaken identity

Birds can be forgiven if now and then they make mistakes in adjusting to the artificial habitats and foods that we have thrust upon them. A downy woodpecker, mistaking a lamppost for a tree, was seen busily pecking away at the steel structure in a Boston park. Even more forgivable was a mockingbird seen trying to remove artificial red berries from a Christmas tree. In much the same way, hummingbirds, which are so enticed by red flowers, are frequently seen exploring other red objects. A red hatpin or red dots on a dress or tie can draw them almost as surely as red salvia. Margaret L. Bodine in National Geographic's *The Book of Birds** tells of a ruby-throated hummingbird that persistently jabbed its bill into the bright-raspberry-red plumage of a male purple finch. But this story was topped by John K. Terres, who tells of a broad-tailed hummingbird in Utah that flew to a traffic light and twice poked its bill against the red light. The bird was not attracted to the green or amber lights at the signal.

That birds mistake soap for food isn't at all surprising. They have no way of knowing its real use, and it looks as much like food as many of the other things we offer them. Around campsites in the West, it is not unusual to have a gray jay or Steller's jay fly off with the only piece of soap in sight. Even the much more sophisticated titmice of the British Isles take a while to learn about

* Margaret L. Bodine, *The Book of Birds* (Washington, D.C.: National Geographic Society, 1932).

soap. In his book on titmice, John Barnes tells of an experiment exposing scented toilet soap at a bird feeder. Titmice of two species had to learn by pecking that the soap wasn't edible.

Marbles can be equally confusing to birds. In California scrub jays have been seen carrying off and burying marbles in much the same way that they would peanuts or acorns. A single pair of scrub jays was observed carrying off fifty marbles in half an hour. In the same way, acorn woodpeckers by way of change of pace sometimes begin hoarding pebbles instead of the customary acorns. Still another example of confusing something else with food is seen in the experience of Laurence J. Webster, a pioneer in bird attracting in New Hampshire. He received painful jabs on several occasions from a red-breasted nuthatch that was coming to his hand for suet but jabbed his finger instead.

When one stops to think of all the foods, not to mention brands, that we are obliged to learn at the supermarket, it is not surprising that birds occasionally make a mistake. They have mastered cold and hot cereals, Jell-O, preserves, cheeses, exotic fruits and nuts, dried fruits, cakes, tarts, buns, and a host of other foods; now they are moving in on the fast-food places where they are learning about pizza, potato chips, french fries, onion rings, pickles, and popcorn. Well-known scavengers like gulls, pigeons, crows, starlings, house sparrows, and grackles are always the first to discover any new source of food. Blue jays are not far behind, and even chickadees, if a few trees are present, are in on the feast. I must admit being surprised, however, when I saw a red-bellied woodpecker awkwardly hopping about on the pavement at a fast-food place at Key Biscayne in Florida. Lured by a newly acquired taste for leftover hotdog rolls, it had flown in some distance from the nearest trees.

The eager way in which birds temporarily forsake natural foods for bread and parking-lot leftovers raises the same question that it does in regard to human use of such foods. Are these foods harmful to the health? Derek Goodwin, in his book *Birds of Man's World*,* offers something in the way of consolation. He notes that beri-beri has virtually disappeared in London's feral pigeons since the enrichment of white bread with added vitamins and minerals.

* Derek Goodwin, *Birds of Man's World* (Ithaca, N.Y.: Cornell University Press, 1978).

That birds so easily recognize the many foods that even sometimes give us trouble is truly astonishing. They master these foods without the assistance of smell, and probably with very little help from taste. They respond well to sweetness, but, on the other hand, are rarely repelled by astringency or what, to our palates, would be the most loathsome of tastes. In addition to color, size, and shape, they seem to select foods on the basis of how much satisfaction they derive from them. If the food goes down well and sits well once down, the bird has an urge to come back for more.

# Water | 3

One of the best and most reliable lures we can offer birds is water. A year-round necessity, water quenches thirst, cools, invigorates, and, a very important consideration, helps keep feathers clean and well groomed. All of this goes a long way toward explaining why the birdbath is such a popular attraction. Although attendance at the birdbath at our farm in Virginia did not equal that at the nearby feeding stations, there was the compensation of greater variety. During watches, which lasted from a few minutes to half a day, I observed no less than seventy-five species coming to drink, bathe or do both. This was thirty more species than counted at the feeding stations. I am speaking of a period of roughly three years between 1964 and 1967. During this time, I put in slightly over two hundred hours of birdbath watching. I am glad that I made this effort, for I discovered that you learn almost as much about birds watching them at water as you do watching them eat.

Our location, a house in a clearing on a high wooded bluff overlooking the Potomac, seemed unusually favorable for good results at the birdbath.

This part of Maryland and Virginia, so filled with beauty and memories of the Civil War, is also rich in birdlife. Ducks idly floating down the river or suddenly rising from the water and moving off in an opposite direction were one of the many rewards of a stroll along the riverbanks. At times during spring and fall, the trees were filled with small birds passing through on their seasonal migrations. Always a few would find the birdbath.

The presence of water below the bluff and a trickling brook in a ravine nearby did not seem to detract from the popularity of my infinitely lesser supply. I suppose the location of my baths (I had two of them) a few feet apart at a point where the lawn merged with forest helped explain their popularity. Birds always respond well to edge effect. The situation was open enough to attract semi-open-country birds, like field and chipping sparrows. At the same time, the bordering woodland assured the presence of a long list of forest dwellers. The only drawback was that we were too closed in by forest to offer adequate habitat for open-country birds like meadowlarks.

### The birdbath

I am afraid that most people regard the birdbath primarily as a yard ornament. As a result the bath doesn't get the attention it deserves. Not having a cat problem and finding that a bath near the ground attracts more birds, I took my birdbaths down from their pedestals and placed them on rock foundations. The baths were in a location protected from strong winds and where they could

*The location of birdbaths in my Virginia yard*

be viewed from my study window. A large American holly offered adequate cover for birds waiting to bathe or those that, having completed their ablutions, were beginning to preen and dry themselves. Immediately beyond the holly, birds had another good source of cover in the form of a medium-sized pine tree.

If at all possible, I like to keep the birdbath well removed from the feeding station. In this way there is less confusion and less chance of shier species being frightened away. Another consideration is that fewer sunflower hulls and other debris fall into the water.

My rough concrete baths, gradually sloping to the deepest points in the middle, which were about two and a half inches, were designed to overcome fears of smaller, more timid birds. Many birds can be tempted to bathe only if the water is very shallow and the footing secure. Of course, not enough water in the bath will also discourage birds. I always try to keep my baths reasonably full, as well as scrubbed and supplied with fresh water. Finally, there is the problem of ice in winter that can cause a temporary closedown. I overcome this problem by keeping electric immersible water heaters in the baths during periods of very cold weather. I am rewarded by birds using the baths the year round. Almost as many birds come in winter as at other times of the year.

Not essential but helpful in announcing the presence of water is a water-drip.* The steady rhythmical splash of drops of water from a bucket or hose falling onto the surface of the birdbath acts as a lure. Birds from near and far come to investigate. I attributed part of my success with warblers to always having a water-drip in use during the migration seasons. Although warblers seemed charmed by the sight of falling water, they did not always gain courage enough to drink or bathe.

The only other feature deserving mention was the concrete pedestal that formerly held one of the baths. For no good reason, I left it standing a few feet from one of the baths. To my surprise, birds began visiting the pedestal in order to bathe in a small circular depression at the top. Slightly over three inches in diameter and three-fourths of an inch deep, this mini-bath was used for bathing whether it held water or not. More on this later.

---

* For details see John Dennis, *A Complete Guide to Bird Feeding* (New York: Alfred A. Knopf, 1975), chapter 5.

One of the first things I noticed in my study of birdbath habits was that birds either come to drink or drink and bathe, almost never only to bathe. The routine is almost always the same. The bird arrives, looks about hesitantly, and then begins drinking. After it drinks, the bird either leaves, or, after some hesitation, enters the water. The bath begins gingerly with a few flicks of the wings and perhaps a peck or two at the water. As the bird gains confidence, it begins to bathe with more enthusiasm. The performance begins with the bird's ducking its head and forebody under, all the while vibrating the wings in such a manner as to splash water over the rest of its body. Almost immediately the head comes up again, the wings continue splashing a bit more, and the first real wetting of the bath is over. Hardly has the bird looked around to see if any danger is in sight when down goes the head and forebody for another round. These quick dips may be repeated many times. They are sometimes accompanied by rolling motions of the fore-regions.

The bird does not necessarily confine itself to one spot while bathing. A vigorous bather may flap about from one part of the bath to another. When a number of birds are bathing together at a time, there is such a seething mass of feathers and spray that it is difficult to see what is taking place. One gets the impression that birds love to bathe as much as we do. Bathing can be a communal activity, with an entire flock participating, some waiting while others bathe, or it can be a solitary venture involving only one bird. Bathing can be mixed, with more than one species in the bath at a time, or bathers can all belong to the same species. Regardless of the makeup of the bathing party, there is normally less squabbling and jockeying for position than at feeding stations.

The real purpose of the bath seems to be to thoroughly drench the skin and feathers for both the cleansing effect and as an aid to easing skin discomfort associated with new feather growth. Of course, we can't rule out the added possibility that birds bathe for the pleasure of it.

After a vigorous session of splashing, the bird, often looking thoroughly bedraggled, emerges and makes for the nearest cover. Here, in safe surroundings, the bird begins the drying and grooming process. These sessions may be inter-

rupted by returns to the birdbath for more bathing. Second baths are the rule,
while third and fourth baths are not unusual.

The preening, which is a part of every bath, may last as long as ten or fifteen minutes. The feathers are drawn through the beak in order to squeeze out water and arrange small interlocking parts of the feather known as bar-bules. The bird may also apply oil to the feathers, giving them sheen and water resistance. The beak is used both to withdraw oil from the preen gland at the base of the tail and to apply the oil to the feathers. The only part of the body the bird can't reach with its beak is the head. To overcome this problem, the bird twists its head around in such a way as to be able to rub it against the preen gland. As will be discussed later in this chapter, the discomfort of molt is believed to induce such relief measures as bathing in water and dust, sunning, anting, and scratching.

### Air bathing

Returning to the pedestal with the circular depression in its top, one day in early March I saw a chickadee in this hole going through many of the same motions it would use in bathing. I was struck by the oddity of the performance, since the hole contained no water. Somehow the bird was able to rotate itself (probably by kicking with its feet) so that it spun around almost completing a circuit of 360 degrees, while flicking its wings in the same way it would if bathing in the birdbath only a few feet away. After a brief bath, if that is what it was, the bird hopped out and flew away. But in a minute or so it was back to repeat the same performance.

Over the next several months, I was to see this same kind of bathing repeated many times by chickadees and also tufted titmice and house sparrows. One day in August a Carolina wren entered the hole and went through the same motions—rotating movements accompanied by wing flicking. The baths never lasted more than ten seconds or so, but frequently the bather would come back for second, third, or fourth rounds.

Were birds fearful of entering the real bath and therefore finding a substitute in a "dry" bath nearby? The answer seemed to be *yes*. Either the sight of water or the sight of other birds bathing initiates an irresistible urge to bathe. But the urge might not be strong enough to overcome fears of entering the water. After all, a bird that is wet and busily bathing is easier prey for a cat or small-bird hawk. Then, too, birds, like ourselves, are probably hesitant about entering a different medium.

Actually air bathing, or *in vacuo* bathing, as it is sometimes called, is a fairly common phenomenon that is touched off by the sight of water and other birds bathing in it. If there is no convenient small "bath" for birds, they will sometimes go through all the motions of bathing out on the lawn or somewhere else near the birdbath. At times a bird, after air bathing, will gain courage and go into the birdbath for a normal bath. Also a bird, after having had its normal bath, will sometimes go on to take an air bath. Such instances may be initiated by reluctance to take a second water bath. A convenient hole near the water bath, such as the small depression in the top of the pedestal, seems to release the air-bathing impulse.

The only detail that still bothered me about air bathing was the rotating movement of the bird once it was in the hole in the pedestal. Then one day, looking out my window, I saw eight or nine house sparrows dust bathing in a nearby flower bed. Each bird had dug a small hole for itself and was briskly fluttering its wings and rotating about in its hole. A bird would first rotate in one direction and then in the other. So rotating motions are actually a part of the bathing routine of birds.

### Bathing and preening

Not all birds follow the stereotyped bathing patterns I have described. Doves and pigeons are lackadaisical bathers that spend most of the time in the bath idly standing about and making occasional pecks at the water; sooner or later there will be a spurt of activity in which the bird ducks its head and splashes itself with its wings. After entering the water at my birdbath, two domestic pigeons stood in one spot as though unsure what to do next. After a minute or two, the sun shining warmly on the bath seemed to cause one of the birds to doze off. Later, the birds, still standing in the bath without having bathed, suddenly fell into the sunbathing position, feathers fluffed out, wings partially

open, and heads cocked to one side. This was one of the few times I've seen
sunbathing taking place in such an unexpected situation. Normally birds, like
ourselves, leave the bath before sunning themselves. Pigeons also engage at times
in billing and cooing while in the bath.

Another peculiarity about pigeons is the fine film of gray matter they
leave on the water after bathing. This is oil from patches of downy feathers
which are known as "powderdowns" and are found chiefly in herons, bitterns,
hawks, and the pigeons and doves. The bill is run through the patches in order
to obtain the lubricant; this, in turn, is applied to the feathers as a cleaning
agent and for waterproofing.*

Hummingbirds are as fond of water and bathing as are other birds. If
they can find fine spray or drops of water to fly through, they usually bathe
on the wing. They take advantage of such opportunities as raindrops, mist
from waterfalls, and spray from garden sprinkler systems. They also flutter
about in wet foliage and sometimes bathe in more conventional fashion by
alighting at a shallow place in a running stream where the water isn't much
deeper than their tiny legs. Ruby-throats at my bird bath chiefly confined
themselves to flying through the water-drip. Once I saw a bird hovering low
enough over the bath to wet itself.

Phoebes, kingbirds, and other flycatchers bathe by flying down from a
perch, hitting the water with the breast, and, without alighting, returning to
the perch. The feat is accomplished so quickly that the observer is scarcely
aware of what is taking place. The performance may be repeated several times
in succession. Back at the perch the bird shakes itself, fluffs out its feathers,
and begins preening. The eastern phoebe sometimes comes to water and bathes
like other birds. One day, as I watched at the banks of the river below us, a
pair of phoebes, stationed at a limb out over the water, began making their
typical breast-splashing dives. Soon several cardinals and warblers of two or
three species, following the example of the phoebes, began bathing at the river's
edge. No matter where it is, the sight of birds bathing is infectious. Other birds
quickly follow suit.

The quick jump in and jump out are employed not only by timid human

---

* For details on powderdown feathers see John K. Terres, *The Audubon Society Encyclopedia of North
American Birds* (New York: Alfred A. Knopf, 1980), pp. 280–1.

bathers but also by tufted titmice and chickadees. These small birds seem as eager to bathe as any of the birds that come to our bath. But it is only after much hesitation and flitting about the edge that they gain nerve to go all the way in. Soon the bather is out, and, if able to talk, might be complaining about how cold the water was. The bath may be repeated several times. A tufted titmouse at my bath took as many as eight baths in about that many minutes. Occasionally a tufted titmouse becomes so thoroughly soaked that it has difficulty flying.

Wrens also go in for quick baths. A Carolina wren literally propelling itself across the bath from one side to the other and back again may not have even touched bottom. Yet the bird was thoroughly soaked when it emerged. Much the same kind of performance took place on the rare occasion when a winter wren visited my bath.

The brown thrasher begins its bath in such a timid way that one wonders if it will even get its toes wet. After much hesitation, it finally enters the water and begins bathing in such an unrestrained fashion that I begin to have a

*Cedar waxwings are vigorous bathers.*

different opinion of the bird. Normally, the brown thrasher is a retiring,
solitary bird that pays only the briefest calls to the birdbath or feeding station.

The cedar waxwing, next on my guest list, almost always appears in
sizable flocks. When the flock arrives at the birdbath, individuals crowd around
the edge and immediately settle down to drinking. Generous amounts of water
are scooped up with each dip of the bill. As the head is raised, some of the
water falls out of the bill, wetting breast and head feathers. The feel of sudden
wetness may act as an incentive to enter the bath and obtain a thorough soak-
ing. It isn't long, as a rule, before one of the birds ventures out into the water
and commences bathing. Others follow this bird's example and soon the birdbath is full of splashing waxwings. There is never any pushing or crowding,
which is typical of these gentle birds regardless of what they happen to be
doing. After a bird has finished its bath, it flies directly up from the water and
away, which is in contrast to most birds. The usual procedure is to return to
the rim and leave from there. Always careful to take turns, waxwings at the
edge of the bath wait for departures before entering the bath themselves.

The vireos, uncommon guests at my bath, bathe by making breast splashes
in much the same manner as flycatchers; they also dash from one side of the
bath to the other by a means of propulsion I've never been able to fathom.

In spite of claims that cardinals are reluctant bathers, I have found birds
of both sexes using my baths for drinking and bathing at all seasons. The only
peculiarity in behavior is a tendency to bathe alone. After its bath, the cardinal
promptly leaves and finds a safe place to begin preening. Bathing, as well as
drinking, is indulged in through the day as well as very early and very late.
These early and late sessions have a counterpart at the feeder, where early and
late dining is the rule with cardinals. In January, a cardinal was drinking at the
birdbath at such a late hour that I had difficulty distinguishing the bird with
my field glasses. Twilight hours have their advantages. There is apt to be less
competition from other birds at this time of the day and it is safer from the
standpoint of small-bird hawks and other diurnal predators.

Of all the birds visiting my Virginia birdbath, none bathed more often
than the chipping sparrow. Bathing occurred on 70 percent of its visits to the
bath during the period from mid-April to late November when the sparrows
were in residency. The next most active bather, in proportion to number of

visits, was the white-throated sparrow. Appearing about the time chipping sparrows leave, white-throats were recorded bathing on 44 percent of their visits. Most other visitors, including tufted titmouse, Carolina chickadee, house sparrow, and cardinal, took baths on far fewer of their visits.

### Bathing by starlings and house sparrows

Among the less welcome visitors to the birdbath are starlings and house sparrows. Starlings, the more tumultuous of the two, arrive in a flock and quickly gather around the rim of the bath to begin drinking. Each bird dips its bill in with a sliding motion, getting the head and breast feathers wet in the process. As bills are raised (often in unison) some of the water falls out, splattering the plumage still more. Heads are tilted back so that the water goes down more easily. After each swallow there is normally a vigorous shake of the head. One gets the impression that the birds are not fond of water and are drinking it only out of a sense of duty. However this may be, the drinking process is soon over and the flock will either fly away or enter the water for a round of bathing.

Normally, it takes only one bird wading out into the water to bring on an infectious rush by others pell-mell into the water. All begin ducking their heads and splashing themselves with their wings. So much spray is raised that sometimes house sparrows (which always keep a watchful eye on anything starlings are doing) come crowding around the edge of the bath to get a shower. They seem to enjoy shower bathing as much as being in the water. In the meantime, the starlings in the bath are beginning to reveal their usual cantankerousness. Uttering shrill bleating noises and turning on each other with wide gaping beaks, they begin to combine fighting with bathing. The flock soon becomes a boiling mass of tumbling, splashing birds. There are never any signs of birds hurting each other; therefore one must assume that this is just part of a game starlings always indulge in. They seem to fight for the love of it.

As the bath continues, some birds begin to leave by flying directly up from the water like waxwings and away. If there are any others waiting, these will immediately crowd into the bath to take their place. Upon departing, birds go to a convenient perch to begin preening operations. This is an animated undertaking, feathers fluffed out, birds shaking themselves, wings opening and closing. The purpose at first seems to be getting rid of excess water. Next the feathers are thoroughly groomed. Occasionally starlings become so soaked by their bath that they are unable to fly. If pursued when in this condition, they

*House sparrows
disporting themselves
in a rain puddle*

try to escape by dodging into the nearest dense cover. Given time to dry and preen, they are soon on the wing again. As with a good many other birds, starlings often bathe in rainy or humid weather.

When starlings have completed their bath, they leave behind the same untidy mess that they do at the feeding station. Most of the water will be splashed out of the bath and what little is left will be contaminated by feathers and droppings.

In spite of their messy habits the birds keep themselves extremely well groomed. Besides frequent bathing in water, followed by much preening, starlings conduct other "bathing" by placing ants in their feathers, letting the rays of the sun get to their skin and feathers, and even allowing themselves, with their feathers fluffed out, to be enveloped by clouds of smoke. The purpose of these other types of bathing, as well as water bathing, is now thought to be associated with the relief of skin irritation caused by feather molt, a topic that will be discussed in more detail. In any case, the starling is fastidious in the way it takes care of its plumage.

House sparrow bathing behavior is so like that of the starling that one would think the two species were related. This of course is far from the case. Starlings belong to the myna (or starling) family, while house sparrows belong to the weaver finches. Both are Old World species brought to this country during the last century with high hopes that the birds would help rid us of insect pests. The starling has proved to be more helpful in this regard than the house sparrow. The two species harm native birdlife, compete for room at bird feeders and bird-baths, litter pavements and windshields with droppings, and keep us awake. One wonders how introduction enthusiasts could have been so unforeseeing as to have brought these two birds to our shores as well as to other parts of the world.

To console myself, I take the view that, since the birds are here to stay, I might as well get as much instruction and entertainment from them as possible. I can safely say that I learn more about bird behavior by observing starlings and house sparrows than I do from equal exposure to native birds. What is more, I find a great deal of amusement in their antics.

If anything, house sparrows are more addicted to taking baths than are the starlings. Any puddle, regardless of how dirty it may be, prompts them

to begin splashing about in a carefree manner. Once engaged in bathing, house
sparrows lose some of their characteristic wariness and begin frolicking in the
water as though thoroughly enjoying themselves. They employ the same wing-
flicking and head-ducking motions that other birds do. Nearly always, bathing
is a communal affair. The ornithologist Frank Chapman observed as many
as four hundred house sparrows bathing at one time in a puddle in Central
Park. This was early in the century before the house sparrow had begun to
decline so sharply in numbers.

The bath is followed by a busy session of preening and perhaps still more
baths and still more preening. Sometimes the next bath is a dust bath. House
sparrows, along with gallinaceous birds—such as grouse and quail—wrens, and
brown thrashers, are among the few dust bathers that visit our yards. Barnyard chickens bathe only in dust, never in water.

Breaking up the soil with their beaks, house sparrows create small craters
in places like flower beds. These dusting places become semi-permanent in
nature. When dusting, the birds use the same wing and head motions that they do

*House sparrows dust bathing*

when bathing in water, only this time it is loose dirt and not water that they douse themselves with. When dusting, the birds rotate in their individual holes in the same way they do when air bathing in a depression of some kind. Birds are quite possessive about rights to individual dusting holes and are quick to drive off any other sparrow that approaches too closely.

As if water and dust bathing were not enough to keep skin and feathers in shape, house sparrows, either independently of other bathing or as a sequel to it, sometimes engage in sunbathing. Picking a sunny spot, as likely as not the same soft ground where dust bathing takes place, birds sprawl out flat on their bellies with wings partly or fully extended and body feathers fluffed out. Lying blissfully this way for many minutes, these hyperactive sparrows at last give the appearance of being relaxed.

Not to omit any other kinds of bathing by this supposedly "untidy" bird, there are reports of house sparrows bathing in melting snow, dusting themselves amid ants in anthills, and entering a factory eating place in England to dust in sugarbowls on dining-room tables.

### Water in summer

It has been shown that mourning doves drink four times as much water at 100 degrees Fahrenheit as they do at 70 degrees. Much of this extra water intake is used for cooling. Since the feathers prevent loss of heat from the skin, evaporation takes place mostly internally. When the environmental temperature reaches 105–107 degrees Fahrenheit, a bird usually begins to pant. This helps increase the flow of air over internal surfaces of the respiratory system.* When birds are inactive on very hot days, they are likely to elevate their wings slightly in order to keep them away from the body. This would prevent the wing feathers from adding still more warmth to the body, and, at the same time, allow more air circulation on the surfaces normally covered by the wings. When the air temperature was 95 degrees Fahrenheit, I noticed that a brown thrasher in my yard held its wings away from its body and had its feathers fluffed out. These were measures that would allow more air to reach the surface of the bird's body.

* See John K. Terres, *The Audubon Society Encyclopedia of North American Birds,* pp. 491–2.

Birds also seek shade in order to keep cooler on hot, sunny days. When driving across the plains of South Dakota on a very hot day one summer, I passed stretches of roadside where a western meadowlark was in the shadow of nearly every fence post. Also to ward off the heat, the birds were holding their wings slightly away from their bodies. The most popular months at the birdbath were October through January and the month of April. In January, the busiest month of all, I recorded an average of one visit to the bath every one and a half minutes. In contrast, during July, the poorest month for attendance, I recorded only one visit every seven minutes.

I must hasten to say that others have observed a different seasonal pattern at their birdbaths. For example, Eloise Potter of Zebulon, North Carolina, writes me that over a three-year period, April through July were the busiest months at her birdbaths. July was always an exceptionally busy month.

Why these differences? I am convinced that attendance at the birdbath is influenced to a large degree by the number of birds coming to nearby feeding stations. When feeders are well attended there are not only more birds in the vicinity but thirstier birds. Almost certainly many of our foods, like sunflower and suet mixtures, make birds thirsty. Without these foods in summer and fewer birds at the feeders anyway, I could hardly expect good attendance at my birdbaths. Statistics aside, the fact remains that birds need water the year round. In winter besides needing water for drinking, birds need it for feather care. The feathers have to be clean and well groomed if they are to retain their insulating properties. Hence birds bathe in winter to keep warm.

When water in the birdbath reaches air temperature on hot summer days, birds seem more reluctant than ever to come to birdbaths. After the sun becomes a little lower in mid-to late afternoon, there is a pickup in activity. The warmest temperatures that birds seemed to tolerate were between 93 and 95 degrees F. On days this hot, there were occasional periods of drinking and bathing. In contrast, one day in late August when the air temperature dropped to 74 degrees, there was a rush of activity that lasted most of the day. Cooler days in summer, I noted many times, were the best for good birdbath attendance.

It helps in summer to change water at frequent intervals. If the water is cool and fresh, birds are much more likely to visit the birdbath. I keep my baths in semishade and use a water-drip for its cooling effect.

*The bath in molting season*

Bathing is only a secondary activity at the birdbath. Most visits are for a drink. On a yearly average, about 30 percent of the visits by birds to my baths culminated in a bath. The percentage of visits for bathing was a little higher in August and September and again in May. Bathing reached its lowest level during the three months February, July, and December.

In trying to interpret these patterns, I have looked into the two molt periods as a partial answer. Birds lose their feathers and grow new ones at least once a year. It is a slow process, with replacement taking place at a pace that keeps up with losses. In this way, the bird is never without feathers and never without the power of flight. Exceptions to this last rule occur in loons, grebes, swans, geese, and ducks. During their postnuptial molt these waterbirds lose so many flight feathers all at once that they are temporarily incapable of flying. Nothing this drastic occurs in small land birds. A partial molt occurs in some species in May, whereas a complete molt takes place in most birds in August and September. In some the molt begins earlier than this.

It is during this period of late-summer molt that birds seem most in need of water. Old accounts in *Bird-Lore,* going back to as early as 1921, tell of birds showing distress during the late summer molt. Feverish, weak, and silent, according to one account, birds find relief by coming to water for extra drinking and bathing. The idea that birds are under stress during the molt period and seek relief through extra drinking and bathing has been revived by several recent workers. As we shall see in the next chapter, anting is also regarded as a type of bathing and is indulged in most intensively during the molt period.

In anting, a bird either passively allows biting ants to crawl through its feathers or actively applies ants to certain of the feather tracts. Birds also apply walnut juice, orange peel, sumac berries, and other substances to their feathers. Many of these applications, including the acid in ants, are likely counter-irritants. Water would not have the same tonic effect. However, a vigorous bath followed by a long session of preening might be an antidote of sorts. There is still much that we do not know about anting and the reasons for it. But a connection between anting and bathing, whether sunbathing, dust bathing, or water bathing, seems probable, and it is equally probable that the molt period is involved in some way.

### Snow and cold temperatures

The only time when the birdbaths were not well attended during winter and early spring was when snow was on the ground. Our period of greatest snow cover in northern Virginia is during February and March. It was during these two months that birdbath attendance reached one of its lowest points.

When snow is on the ground, birds have another source of moisture. They eat snow to quench their thirst, and even bathe in snow. Chickadees cling to icicles and drink water that has collected at the tips. As the snow melts, puddles form, and these provide additional bathing and drinking places. During warm spells in winter, it is not uncommon to see birds bathing in roadside puddles. There are so many sources of water that the birdbath may become temporarily deserted. But with a hard freeze, and especially if there is no snow on the ground, birds are grateful for any unfrozen water they can find.

*Dripping icicles are a source of water for thirsty chickadees in winter.*

Always the busiest periods of drinking and bathing at my baths are when water is first made available.

Bathing in very cold weather is not without its risks. Starlings bathing when the air temperature was slightly above zero became encased in ice and couldn't fly. Worse yet, a starling that braved a heated birdbath when the temperature was 10 degrees below zero was found dead twenty feet away, apparently having frozen to death. On the other hand, evening grosbeaks seem able to bathe in subzero weather without ill effect. A white-throated sparrow bathing at my birdbath when the air temperature was only 16 degrees seemed none the worse for the experience. A cardinal wintering in Michigan braved a chill 20 degrees to take a bath. When the air temperature hovers between 23 and 26 degrees, birds begin to bathe as actively as ever at my baths. The cool air does not dampen their ardor.

Downy woodpeckers, crows, horned larks, black-capped chickadees, juncos, and white-throated sparrows have been observed bathing in snow. They make the same head-ducking motions and wing vibrations that accompany water bathing.

Ice is a much more difficult problem for birds than snow. Many a chill morning I have looked out and watched birds pecking at the frozen surface of the birdbath or simply standing on the ice and looking about in a melancholy way. This is all the reminder I need to get a kettle of hot water and start thawing operations.

When a swimming pool at a home where we were staying began to freeze over, a male cardinal daringly landed on the razor-thin ice and began to look for a place to drink. With each step the bird took, the ice was seen to buckle. Reaching a small opening, the bird took a drink and then flew away. A flicker, finding a birdbath in a Denver yard frozen over, was undeterred. It began drilling into the ice with its sharp beak and eventually reached water. The thickness of the ice was about half an inch. A blue jay was equally resourceful when it found the birdbath in a Michigan yard empty except for a rim of ice around the edge. The bird began chipping away at the ice with its beak and eating the small pieces it broke off. This blue jay or another came back a few days later to repeat the performance.

Ice-eating may be fairly widespread among jays. There is an account in

Bent's *Life Histories* of a Steller's jay in Colorado hammering at frozen patches of snow and swallowing the icy fragments it broke off. The habit is not limited to jays. Even juncos have been seen chipping off pieces of frozen snow and eating the ice crystals.

### Rain

The best attendance at the bath in late summer and early fall was always on cooler days. A threat of rain also seemed to act as a stimulus, bringing more birds to the bath. The greatest flurry of activity was when the first drops of rain began to fall. The feel of wetness on their feathers sends birds to the bath in much the same way that soaked clothing sends us to the tub or shower. This is true only if rain comes after a dry spell. Prolonged rainy weather has the opposite effect and dampens any enthusiasm for bathing.

It takes only a few raindrops following dry weather to stimulate the bathing response in brown thrashers, robins, starlings, cardinals, purple finches, goldfinches, white-throats, and song sparrows, to name a few of the birds that seem to bathe most often in the rain. One December day in Florida, I saw flocks of robins bathing in puddles along the roadsides in the midst of a hard downpour. Of course, robins also rejoice in the aftermath of a good rain—the earthworms that come to the surface when the ground becomes wet.

Many birds bathe in wet foliage during or after a rain. This is particularly true during a summer shower. Foliage that is wet from dew will also stimulate bathing. Whether bathing in wet leaves, grass, or foliage of other plants, birds use the same head-ducking and wing-vibrating motions that are seen when they are bathing in water. But it is a much more uninhibited kind of bathing. The bird may flutter about in one clump of foliage and then go to another. Anyone seeing such a performance might well wonder what the bird was up to.

A hairy woodpecker was seen bathing in a novel way during a rain shower. Clinging to the side of a house at a spot where a gutter overflowed, it bathed by letting the water tumble over its plumage. This was not a completely passive performance, for the bird also fluffed out its feathers and flicked its wings.

*Drinking*

Most birds drink by taking water in the beak and then tilting the head back. Exceptions are hummingbirds, pigeons and doves, sandgrouse, and certain of the grass finches of Australia. Hummingbirds, regardless of the angle of the bill, can draw liquid in through their partly tubular tongues. The other birds mentioned can drink without tilting back by drawing water in through the lowered bill. It is interesting to watch the differences between members of the pigeon family and other birds at the birdbath. A mourning dove will lower its head and suck in water for a few seconds, raise its head, look around, and go back to further drinking with the head lowered. Most other visitors to the birdbath will down their drinks in much the same way that a female flicker did at my bath. After arriving at the rim of the bath, she looked around in all directions to make sure that no danger was lurking. Then, inserting her long bill well into the water, she filled it and immediately lifted her head to where the bill pointed upward at an angle of 45 degrees. After swallowing, she looked around nervously for a moment and then went back to drinking again. She took between ten and thirteen drinks or swallows per visit. I thought this amount of water somewhat excessive until I began counting the number of drinks taken by other visitors to the birdbath.

A yellow-bellied sapsucker took six drinks while a purple finch took seven. The maximum number of drinks taken by brown thrashers and cardinals was eleven. A mockingbird bested the flicker by taking fourteen quick drinks. Both a downy and red-bellied woodpecker exceeded this number by taking fifteen drinks. But a robin surpassed all the other birds by taking well over twenty drinks!

To be sure, it is not so much the number of drinks that counts but how many times the bird comes back for more water. While data on this point are scanty, random observations lead me to believe that some birds return to drink many more times a day than others. Starlings, cedar waxwings, evening grosbeaks, and robins, for example, come frequently to water. But, except for the robin, they drink only small amounts at one time.

Thirst seems correlated with the kind of food a bird eats. For its size, the

American goldfinch, whose diet consists almost entirely of plant food, seems to
require more water than most other North American birds. The government
wildlife biologist F. E. L. Beal, who conducted so many food-habit studies early
in this century, stated that he had seen more goldfinches drinking in one day
than he had seen all other species in his whole life. While this may sound like
an exaggeration, I can vouch for the fact that goldfinches were by far the most
common birds drinking at ponds, rivers, and streams in the northern Virginia
area where we lived. Goldfinches are also great bathers and just as apt to bathe
in rainy weather as when the sun is shining.

There is something about a largely vegetarian diet that creates a strong
thirst. It isn't clear whether vegetarians drink so much because of the dryness
of their food, especially seeds, or because the extra water is needed as an aid to
digestion.

Still another reason for vegetarians to drink more than other birds is the
astringency of many fruits and berries. Common names like chokeberry and
chokecherry tell us something of the unpleasant reaction that people have

*Chokecherries make birds thirsty.*

when tasting certain fruits. But no matter how astringent or bitter certain fruits are, birds seem undaunted. The chokecherry (*Prunus virginiana*) is in such demand when in season between July and September that birds can't seem to eat enough of the puckery fruits. After a session of feeding, they descend to the nearest pond, stream, or birdbath to quench an unusually violent thirst.

When spending the winter in South Carolina, I had to refill my birdbath at frequent intervals when large flocks of robins and starlings were in the vicinity. Soon after eating fruits still on trees in late fall and early winter, the birds, apparently intensely thirsty, would appear at the bath to begin a round of drinking and bathing. The pits and seeds they regurgitated and left in and around the birdbath told me what they had been eating. Looming importantly in their diets were fruits of red cedar, glossy privet, black gum, greenbrier, yaupon (*Ilex vomitoria*), and wax myrtle. This was a combination that could have easily driven birds to drink!

Peanut butter may have the same effect upon the thirst as astringent fruits. No longer recommended for bird feeding because it sometimes clogs the windpipes of chickadees, peanut butter is both salty and sticky. This is good reason why birds seem to crave water after eating it. Common grackles have been seen carrying peanut butter to a birdbath for dunking before flying on to the nest to offer it to their young.

Food dunking is sometimes carried to extremes by grackles. They commonly dunk not only bakery products in water but also seeds, fruits, and almost anything they eat. Stale bread and, yes, pieces of doughnut are dunked and sometimes left in water until the proper consistency for eating has been attained. Wetting helps the food go down, and, at the same time, assuages thirst. Grackles even leave something in the birdbath by way of exchange (?) for the food that has been dunked and eaten. Grackles coming to my birdbath in Maryland during the nesting season commonly deposited a fecal sac from a nearby nest. Other bits of trash and debris are also left in the bath. At the same time, grackles have a way of tidying up the birdbath. They wade about in the water picking up objects, which they either eat or remove. All in all, grackles are about as tidy as they are messy.

Other birds that dunk food include the starling, house sparrow, red-winged blackbird, and Brewer's blackbird. Nearly always the food is bread or some other bakery product. But yellow-bellied sapsuckers, using natural food and their own sap wells, which they have drilled in the limbs and trunks of trees, carry on a unique kind of dunking operation during the nesting season. Before offering wads of sticky insects to their young, they are known to moisten the bundle at one of their sap wells. Nearly always a habit that seems wholly artificial, such as dunking food at the birdbath, has its counterpart in the wild.

*A red-winged blackbird dunks bread in a birdbath.*

*Typical active anting posture as seen in a blue jay*

# Anting and Related Antics | 4

In the previous chapter, I referred to the strange phenomenon known as anting. Birds either sit on an anthill or in a line of marching ants and allow the ants to crawl through their plumage, or, in active anting, they pick up one or more ants in their bills and use them to anoint their plumage. After the bodily juices of the ant have been distributed through portions of the feathers or on the skin, the insect's by now badly mangled remains are discarded or eaten. Areas receiving this treatment are chiefly the undersides of each wing, the flanks and thighs, and the region around the base of the tail.

Close scrutiny reveals that an ant is taken in the bill and the bird then twists its head far around to reach the more inaccessible parts of its body. To facilitate this action, one folded wing is extended forward so that its tip touches the ground and the tail is bent under in such a way that the bird sometimes steps on it. In this awkward position the bird occasionally loses its equilibrium and falls over on its side or falls backward as though doing a somersault. As in sunning and water bathing, the nictitating membrane often covers the eyes.

Persons seeing an anting bird going through these strange motions not infrequently conclude that the bird is in convulsions or intoxicated. They may try to pick it up. If approached, a bird that is anting will fly away like any other bird. The motions of the bird may also be mistaken for preening or sunbathing.

The ants chosen for this performance are almost exclusively ones that exude or spray formic acid or other strong fluids. This is the number-one clue to the reason or reasons for anting. Birds seem to revel in substances that are hot, penetrating, and, at the same time, pungent or aromatic. It is most likely the feel of these substances and *not* the odor that is the attraction. As we saw earlier, birds have a poorly developed sense of smell.

Little information is available as to whether birds are bitten by ants during anting. In passive anting, the ants have every opportunity to bite their tormentors. Not all ant species, by any means, bite, but some of those known to be used by birds in anting have a bite that can be felt. Between bites (if they do occur) and the acid secretions, the bird may be subjected to two kinds of sensations. The bites could be painful, while the ant's acid might produce a slight burning sensation. Of course, we can't be sure of any of this. The major difficulty in studying anting is that we can't put ourselves in the place of the bird. Our skin is different, and of course we have no feathers.

After first stirring up the ants with its bill, the bird that is passively anting settles down on an ant mound or in the path of ants and fluffs out its feathers. As the rampaging ants stream out of their holes and swarm over the bird, they seem bent upon the destruction of this rude invader. The bird, on its part, takes these attacks calmly enough and even seems to enjoy them. After all, its apparent purpose is to come in as close contact as possible with the ants, or, more precisely, their strong fluids.

Once the bird has allowed itself to be overrun with ants, it is through with their services. After shaking them off and perhaps eating some of them, it may go on to other activities. The anting session is approximately the equivalent of a vigorous rubdown in the human species. It is stimulating, if not painful, but apparently leaves the subject with a sense of well-being. More will be said about the suspected reasons for anting in birds, a topic that is far from settled and that has been debated for some decades.

Something of a mystery surrounds the history of anting. First commented upon by Audubon around 1830, anting didn't figure significantly as a subject of ornithological interest until the mid-1930s. Audubon, who has so many "firsts" to his credit, described how young wild turkeys went to deserted ant-hills in order to rid their feathers of parasites and loose scales. He was probably witnessing dusting, or, just possibly, passive anting. In any event, he passed an astute opinion on what he saw in thinking it had something to do with plumage care.

Why the subject remained almost untouched from Audubon's time until nearly the present needs an explanation. Perhaps the main reason lay in misinterpretation of what the bird was doing. Unless a bird is actually seen picking up ants, the observer could easily conclude that he was watching sunbathing or preening. Passive anting is easily mistaken for dusting. Secondly, anting, especially when compared to bathing in water or sunbathing, is an uncommon activity. Many species of birds never ant at all, and those that do ant only under proper conditions. Anting is primarily a summer and early-fall activity and is almost never seen in wild birds in northern temperate regions during colder months.

Thanks to an Australian named Alec H. Chisholm, anting finally began to get the attention it deserved. Spurred on by the report of a boy in Sydney, who wondered what a starling was doing when it rubbed its plumage with ants, Chisholm decided to launch an all-out investigation. This was in 1934 and

*Passive anting by a robin on a busy ant hill*

in time for him to speak of anting in his book *Bird Wonders of Australia*, published that same year. Earlier, in 1927, Chisholm had received a similar report about a starling anting but let the matter pass.

Through his writings, lectures, and travels, Chisholm took the story of anting to widely separated parts of the world. He was soon rewarded by almost floods of information. Anting hadn't been so completely overlooked after all; it was more that no one had gathered the many reports and unraveled the meaning. Among those who contributed liberally to Chisholm's fund of knowledge were Dr. Erwin Stresemann of the University of Berlin and Roy Ivor, the Canadian ornithologist, who studied anting in captive birds. By the year 1959, when an important article of his on anting appeared in the Australian bird publication, *The Emu*, Chisholm had compiled a world list of 160 bird species known to ant. He could report that about twenty-four ant species were used by birds and about forty substitute materials. His interpretation was that birds anted because of skin stimulation and plumage cleansing.

I have seen only about six or seven anting episodes in thirty years. Nearly all were in yards containing birdbaths and feeding stations. At Moose Hill, I observed a hand-reared common grackle anting soon after it was released. The ant was rubbed three or four times along the flanks or under the wings and then dropped. If it lay motionless, it was picked up again and eaten. During two very hot days in dry weather in late September, I observed a number of anting episodes at my Maryland residence. In all cases, starlings feeding on the lawn were involved. A bird would pick up an ant and in one quick motion rub it under the wing or along the flanks and then go back to feeding. I saw another starling anting episode on the same lawn in May. Again this was a very perfunctory affair and not in keeping with some other descriptions of anting by starlings. Starling anting sessions can be quite uproarious, with birds fighting among themselves for possession of the ants. As the birds begin to ant, they assume odd postures and begin falling over in the manner I have already described. It must be a highly comical performance.

When living on the farm in Virginia, I saw a dark-eyed junco anting on the late date of October 23. This bird went through the odd motions of all-out anting but did not fall over. One wing was stretched out full-length with the tip touching the ground and the tail bent under. When I first saw the bird in this awkward position, I thought it was bathing *in vacuo*, as described in the previous chapter. The birdbath, with birds splashing in it, was only twenty feet away. I observed still another anting episode on this part of the lawn. This time it was midsummer and I was watching a male cardinal feeding a young bird that had been out of the nest maybe two or three weeks. Suddenly the young bird assumed a typical anting posture and went through all the motions. The lawn at this particular spot was alive with ants. According to Margaret Nice, song sparrows may begin to ant at early ages. To her, this was a sign that it was an instinctive reaction.

Although my personal observations of anting have been few, I wouldn't consider myself a below-average anting watcher. A. H. Chisholm, the world's authority, did not see a bird anting until nine years after first becoming intensely interested in the subject. Anting is something that one has to watch for over a period of years. Thanks to the dedicated work of two housewives in North Carolina, we know roughly how many anting episodes to anticipate in a small yard over a period of five or six years.

The late Doris C. Hauser in Fayetteville and Eloise F. Potter in Zebulon looked out of their windows many times daily over astonishingly long periods of time and faithfully recorded every instance of anting they saw in their respective yards. Mrs. Potter recorded fifteen episodes of anting over a period of twenty-nine months. She made at least one observation every two hours daily from 6:00 A.M. until dark. An anting episode might involve only one bird or a number of birds representing several species. In her observations she saw twenty-five birds of six species ant. She later moved to another location near Zebulon where she saw ten anting episodes in two years. Blue jays and starlings were the bird species she saw anting most frequently. She also observed anting in the catbird, robin, house sparrow, and junco.

Mrs. Hauser, also known for her work on sunbathing in birds, recorded forty-eight episodes of anting in six years of watching. She observed anting by thirteen species. Moreover, she made some highly original observations on anting in squirrels, which I shall comment upon later. During the warmer months, when birds ant, both Mrs. Hauser and Mrs. Potter saw an average of between one and two anting episodes a month. Whether their average would hold for other parts of North America is questionable.

In their joint *Auk* contribution,* they suggest that anting occurs most often in the part of the United States where thunderstorms occur on an average of between thirty and fifty days per year. The connection they see between anting and thunderstorms is an interesting one. They state that heavy precipitation causes an almost simultaneous loss of feathers that would have been dropped gradually by a bird in molt had the bird not been exposed to abnormal wetness. As the replacement of these feathers begins, the bird is subject to much more skin discomfort than if the feather loss had been more gradual. As a consequence, the bird that is undergoing sudden new feather growth seeks relief in the form of such activities as scratching, dusting, anting, sunbathing, and water bathing. Each species has its own method or methods of seeking relief. Anting is apparently one of the more uncommon methods.

When a bird is undergoing rapid molt of the head, neck, and upper regions, sunbathing, with its heating effect, according to Potter and Hauser, is more likely to be the choice than anting. Sunbathing is witnessed most often in May and early summer, the time when the postnuptial molt sees feather

* Eloise F. Potter and Doris C. Hauser, "Relationship of Anting and Sunbathing to Molting in Wild Birds," *Auk* 91 (July 1974): 537–63.

*Anting by a young cardinal*

replacement in some birds occurring in the head region and upper extremities. But when rapid molt occurs on the lower breast, under-tail, and under-wing surfaces, something that most often happens in late summer, the bird may resort to anting. It is easier for the bird to expose these lower extremities to ants than to the rays of the sun.

It must be remembered that it took faithful observation and recording over a period of years for Potter and Hauser to arrive at these conclusions. The wonder is that they learned so much solely through watching the birds in their yards. The need at present is for further observations that will test the correctness of their results. If we live anywhere within the thirty-to-fifty-day-per-year thunderstorm belt and are willing to devote ample time and patience to the project, we could very well witness as many anting episodes as did Mrs. Potter in her yard and Mrs. Hauser in hers. The thunderstorm zone in question extends from about South Carolina, Tennessee, and Arkansas north to the Great Lakes and New York City and east from the Great Plains to the Atlantic. Outside this zone, our luck might not be so good. In fact, Mrs. Potter, writing in 1973, states that she knew of no records of anting in wild birds from Florida, New England, or the Pacific Coast region of the United States.

My Massachusetts record of a recently released hand-reared grackle anting would hardly qualify for a place in Mrs. Potter's list. Both she and Mrs. Hauser insisted upon limiting their observations and records to strictly wild birds. It is well known that birds that live in confinement tend to exhibit traits and behavior patterns different from those seen in their wild cousins.

However, one should not rule out the possibility of a fair amount of anting taking place outside the boundaries of the thunderstorm zone. If sudden drenching rains result in rapid molt, the right conditions might occur almost anywhere. Drier parts of the country have their occasional thunderstorms, and the Gulf states have an above-the-average number of summer thunderstorms. So while Potter and Hauser may have discovered the optimum zone for observing anting, we should not rule out both the drier and wetter sections of the country. It could be that the lack of anting records from these other sections reflects more the lack of observers than absence of anting.

Just what the true situation is remains to be seen. But as more people become interested in this subject and begin making observations, a clearer pattern should emerge. Attention should be paid to all other similar activities, including bathing in water, dust, smoke, or the rays of the sun. Conditions prevailing at the time of an anting episode should be noted. Of special importance are weather conditions and the state of the bird's plumage; that is, whether the bird is molting or not. The serious student will also want to know the kind of ants being used and, if it is possible to find this out, whether or not the bird is infested with parasites.

Chisholm did not rule out the possibility that birds ant in order to rid themselves of skin and feather parasites. In his review of anting, John K. Terres reports upon the various theories of why birds ant, but he does not seem to favor any one theory himself. On the whole, however, there seems to be little evidence to support the theory that anting is resorted to by birds as a way of controlling infestations of skin or feather parasites. Potter and Hauser point out that the seasonal peak in anting in this country is in summer, a time of the year when birds are the freest of skin and feather parasites. Moreover, as shown by examinations of birds immediately after they have anted, many are totally free of any external parasites. Although the evidence is as yet incomplete, it would appear that anting has its roots in something other than getting rid of parasites.

In looking for anting activity by birds in our yard, we should conduct our observations in a number of places and not just the lawn. Birds not infrequently pick up ants and fly with them to tree limbs or rooftops. Even the bird feeder is a possible anting site. Perhaps the best advice on where and when to look comes from our two authorities, Mrs. Potter and Mrs. Hauser. They say the key to detecting anting, as well as sunbathing, behavior in wild birds lies not in long hours of observation but in one's knowledge of where to look in one's yard. Once the anthills and favored sunning spots have been located, ten or more one-minute checks throughout the day are more likely to produce results than a full hour once a day. They further advise watching more closely for anting and sunbathing during periods of high humidity, particularly for two or three days after heavy or prolonged rainfall from mid-May through August.

In an article in a 1970 issue of *The Auk,* Mrs. Potter reported that about half the birds she saw anting were definitely undergoing molt and that others may have been molting. Writing to me in August 1980, she tells of witnessing additional anting episodes at her home in Zebulon and notes that nearly all the birds involved were definitely in molt. She goes on to say that water bathing seems to be primarily for loosening feathers during molt periods and that birds, obviously dirty, bathe to get clean and also to prepare for the preening and oiling of feathers. She feels that dusting is a substitute for anting and sunning. All three, anting, sunning, and dusting, she believes, are methods of applying heat to feather tracts during periods of rapid feather growth. The heating effect of formic acid lies in its strong penetrating properties and may feel much like a hot poultice on sensitive skin. When sunbathing, birds fluff out their feathers in a way that allows as much of the sun's rays as possible to reach the bare skin. Needless to say, this is an effective way of applying heat, as is bathing in hot dust. Mrs. Potter's conclusion therefore is that birds find relief from skin irritation through these various heating agents.

*Substitute materials*

It is interesting that, following Audubon, the next reference to anting contained the first report of something other than ants being used. Philip Gosse* told of Antillean grackles anting with limes. It would be hard to find a vegetable material more stingingly penetrating than lime juice. Limes, which are highly acidic, could be expected to give birds the same prickling sensations that formic acid seems to produce. Since Gosse's time, there have been additional reports of birds anting with limes and other citrus fruits. Usually the anting is done with pieces of the rind, since the whole fruit would normally be too large. For example, grackles scavenging in trash baskets at picnic areas and city parks are sometimes seen anting with pieces of orange peel.

Other plant materials used by birds in anting include sumac berries, chokecherries, apple peel, walnut leaves, green fruits of the English walnut, and raw onion. Most of these products are highly acid and would have about the same bite as citrus fruit. Apparently birds discover these substances by means of trial and error.

Chisholm, besides his work on anting, also collected information on insecti-

* Philip Gosse, *Birds of Jamaica* (London, 1847).

cidal plants that birds use in their nests. He reported that house sparrows in Australia mutilated a pyrethrum plant for three successive years in order to gather the foliage for their nests. The plant is the well-known source of an insecticide. Other plants with records of similar use by birds in Australia were lavender cotton, thyme, and common rue. To the list of plants of this kind that birds use in their nests, I can add yarrow, which also has insecticidal properties. On our farm in Virginia, I frequently found fresh sprigs of yarrow in house sparrow nests built in birdhouses.

We perhaps shouldn't go too far in attributing birds with an ability to recognize and make use of insecticidal plants. This ability, if it really exists, would seem to be limited to isolated cases of birds' having chanced upon suitable plants growing nearby and taken the leaves or sprigs to their nests. The house sparrow has shown the most ability as a "botanist," while some credit may be given to the European goldfinches in Australia that used thyme in constructing their nests.

This brings us to another argument in opposition to the view that birds ant in order to rid themselves of external parasites. If they "knew" that ants or their acids helped control these pests (a debatable point), they might be expected to be equally versed in using insecticidal plants on their plumage in the same way they use ants. Plant materials of various kinds are used by birds in anting, but none of them, so far as I am aware, have conspicuous insect-killing properties. This is an argument that occurred to me when reading about materials birds are known to use in disinfecting their nests.

There are reports of other insects besides ants being used in anting, and birds have been known to use such other improbable ingredients as vinegar, beer, hot chocolate, soapsuds, hair tonic, mustard, pickles, and mothballs. Grackles are avid users of the last of these items. One of the many reports is of a flock of around twenty in Milwaukee that was seen coming daily to a vegetable garden. It was discovered that the birds were anting with partly evaporated mothballs put out to discourage rabbits.

The strangest of all strange ingredients used in anting is fire. Chisholm reported anting with lighted cigarettes in the jay and magpie in Europe, and, on this side of the Atlantic, the blue jay. The magpie, a tame bird kept as a pet in England, anted only with the hot end of cigarette butts, never the dead end.

The same was true of a hand-reared blue jay in Texas. Another clever magpie
in England would enter a house with its beak full of ants, fly to the shoulder
of anyone smoking a pipe, dip its beak into the hot ashes, and apply the mixture
to the undersurface of its wings. One can imagine the reaction of the pipe
smoker who was exposed to this performance for the first time!

Maurice Burton, an English writer with the British Museum of Natural
History, topped any accounts of birds anting with fire with his stories of tame
rooks. One, on its own initiative, learned to hold a match in its toes and peck
at the head until it burst into flames. The lighted match was then applied to
the undersides of the wings. Another bird not only anted with lighted matches
but "wallowed" in burning straw. It performed its fire act many times and was
said never to have been burned.

Anting with fire is not unknown in wild birds that have access to burning
cigarettes or cigars. There are rare cases of houses catching on fire or brushfires
resulting from birds taking smoldering materials to their nests. The moral of
the story would seem to be that we must be extra-careful to put out fire on
the chance that a bird will burn our house down.

There are also reports of birds entering clouds of steam or smoke and then
going through the motions of anting. It seems difficult to believe that smoke
could have anything but a highly discomforting effect upon the bird coming
into contact with it. Yet birds seem able to endure short exposure to smoke
without ill effect. They are probably drawn to heat present in smoke and not

*A rook in England learned how to ignite a*
*match and then applied the hot tip to the*
*undersides of its wings.*

anything in the chemical makeup of smoke. As we have already seen, anting in all its many aspects frequently involves some form of heat. It should be remembered that we can't interpret bird behavior on the basis of our own reactions. We wouldn't think of applying ants to our bodies, not to mention fire, or bathing in smoke.

In Europe, smoke bathing has been reported in jackdaws, rooks, and starlings. Care must be taken not to confuse the habit of some birds, especially starlings, of warming themselves by chimneys in cold weather with smoke bathing.

### Comparison with other bathing

When ants are rubbed through the plumage in prolonged anting sessions, the plumage begins to look wet. The bird has literally been bathing in ants. It is a more potent bath than any the bird could take in water, and, as a rule, is not accompanied by preening with oil from the preen or uropygial gland.

Bathing in ants and bathing in water appear to serve much the same purposes. Both give the bird an exhilarating lift and help sooth discomfort. Water bathing has the added function of cleansing and preparation of the feathers for preening. The bird, of course, hasn't thought out all these advantages. Bathing is something that comes naturally, while only a few birds are on to anting and still fewer on to such sophisticated twists as bathing in hot tobacco ash or flames.

Water bathing and anting have something else in common. Both at times inspire air or *in vacuo* bathing, which was described in the previous chapter. The bird acts out all the motions of bathing without either stepping into water or picking up an ant. All that is needed to initiate these strange charades is proper stimuli. Water, with other birds bathing in it, at times induces air bathing in a bird that perhaps is hesitant about getting wet. The sight of ants or other birds anting may have the same effect upon a bird. Only this time it is reluctant to apply ants to its plumage. Edward Armstrong* describes how he saw a starling "go through all the motions of ant-bathing, pecking toward the

---

* Edward Armstrong, *Bird Display and Behaviour* (New York: Oxford U. Press, 1947).

ground and repeatedly putting its bill under its wing without picking up any ants."

Sunbathing, which is seen much more frequently than anting, is yet another way in which a bird exposes its skin and feathers to an outside influence. Heat is the agent that seems to touch off sunbathing. Birds sunbathe much more often in hot weather than they do in cool weather. The full force of the sun's rays is needed to bring on a spell of sunbathing. Doris C. Hauser, whom I've already referred to so often, conducted a series of observations in her Fayetteville yard on sunbathing in birds. In an article in a 1957 issue of *The Wilson Bulletin,* she tells of birds in her yard sunbathing in a variety of situations but always in full sun. One of the most popular sunning sites was a compost heap. Birds also sunbathed on a window feeding tray exposed to the full rays of the sun, on the driveway, on a heap of drying magnolia leaves, and on limbs of trees. She observed sunbathing most often when the clouds lifted after a rain shower or on a bright sunny day following a period of rainy weather. Birds were observed to sunbathe when the temperature at the sunning site was as high as 140 degrees F.

She suggested that birds sometimes seemed to be overpowered by the strength of the sun's rays, and, no longer in complete control of their reactions, sprawled out in a sunbathing position. She called this involuntary sunbathing. The more normal sunbathing seen so often in birds she called voluntary sunbathing. Whatever the case may be, the sunbathing bird for a while seems as blissfully absorbed in what it is doing as the bird that is anting or bathing in water. Either lying flat on its belly or on its side, it may have one or both wings outstretched, the tail fanned, the feathers fluffed out, bill partly open as though panting, and nictitating membrane usually over the eyes. The bird may stay rigidly in this position for many minutes. Although seemingly in a trance, it quickly flies off if disturbed or threatened by danger.

In early summer, Mrs. Hauser observed more young birds sunbathing than adults. In late summer, it was the other way around, with many adults in all stages of the molt sunning themselves and following this activity with a session of preening. The bird that has sunbathed may also go to the nearest water for a bath. But unlike the height of bird anting, which coincided with the late-summer molt, sunbathing among Mrs. Hauser's resident birds occurred most frequently during the two months immediately preceding the peak in anting activity. As has already been pointed out, sunbathing has as much to do with the molt as anting.

Sunbathing, as Mrs. Hauser indicated, can take place in almost any spot that is exposed to the full rays of the sun. I've had birds in my yard sunbathe on the lawn, at bird feeders, and even on the top of a birdhouse. I've mentioned the domestic pigeons which used my birdbath to bathe, sunbathe, and make love, combining all three activities during one session. A red-winged blackbird, at my birdbath in South Carolina, began sunbathing when only halfway out of the water. It is not unusual for birds to fly from a birdbath to a sunny spot and begin to sunbathe. After a session of sunning the bird may be back for another water bath.

Sometimes the water bath is followed by a dust bath (especially in house sparrows). Birds at times dry their feathers in the sun after a hard downpour. This I've seen turkey vultures do on many occasions. Looking like scarecrows, perched in dead trees or on roofs of abandoned houses, they spread their wings

*Turkey vulture sunbathing*

and let the sun dry their damp feathers. Mrs. Potter writes me that turkey vultures in dry weather, and also starlings, sometimes perch on hot tin roofs absorbing the heat. While undergoing their heat baths, the starlings often wave their wings.

Although reasons given for sunbathing in birds range from relief of skin irritation during the molt period to production of vitamin D, there is really no proof that birds consciously expose themselves to the sun for these reasons or, to mention still another theory, to induce ectoparasites to go to areas where the bird can more easily remove them. However, birds, like ourselves or our dog or cat, may expose themselves to the sun for the sheer pleasure of it. Most of us will admit to a feeling of bliss or well-being when the sun reaches parts of our body that rarely receive its rays. If we receive some benefits to our health or cure an itch, so much the better.

If it is heat that stimulates sunbathing in birds and leads them to expose themselves so often to the sun and to indulge in such orgies as bathing in flames and anting with lighted matches or cigarettes, why is it that birds for the most part avoid the midday sun? This is the quietest time of the day for bird activity. As the sun climbs in the sky, bird song diminishes and more and more birds seek out the shade. Fortunately, we now have a clue to this riddle. As we have seen, heat is believed to be the principal agent in relieving irritation caused by feather molt. Certainly not all birds seen sunning themselves or in exposed places on hot, sunny days are having molt problems, but it seems reasonable to believe that many of them are.

## Other anting

A. H. Chisholm, in his pioneer work on anting in birds, uncovered examples of anting in a wholly different group of animals. Several of his correspondents in Australia began writing to him about house cats using ants in somewhat the same way birds do. With outward signs of delight, cats were observed rubbing ants into their fur; in one case, a cat spent a long time licking an ant-infested log. Cats even began rolling with obvious joy in ant debris emptied from an entomologist's collecting case.

These accounts remind us of the way cats revel in the aromatic foliage of catmint (*Nepeta cataria*) and also cat thyme (*Teucrium marum*). Cats cavort and roll in the foliage of these plants and also eat the leaves. Not to be over-looked is the somewhat similar behavior in dogs when they are seen rolling in excrement or decaying matter.

Now that the cat had been identified with anting, it could be expected that other examples would follow. It wasn't long before the gray squirrel of North America was added to the list. Two records of anting by squirrels were obtained in the early 1950s. One involved a gray squirrel, while the animal in the other anting episode was identified only as a "timber" squirrel. Additional examples of anting by gray squirrels were reported by Mrs. Hauser in a 1964 *Journal of Mammalogy*. Once again her yard was the scene of a little-known activity. In early July, young gray squirrels began displacing birds at sunbathing and dusting areas. The squirrels also discovered ant mounds used by birds in passive anting. Like the anting bird at these sites, the squirrel would disturb the ants by digging into the mound and then sprawl out to "enjoy" the results. The excited capers of anting squirrels, when presumably bitten in tender places, outdid anything seen in birds under similar conditions. The squirrel, according to Mrs. Hauser, would suddenly leap into the air, turn somersaults, and roll over and over. So addicted did the squirrels become to this form of entertainment that they soon had their special anting sites that they jealously guarded from other squirrels.

### A plausible explanation

If anting is such a pleasurable activity in cats and squirrels, why not in birds? Birds differ in having feathers and they are further removed from us phylogenetically; therefore we may have a harder time understanding their motives and emotions. But increasingly students, including the noted German behaviorist Konrad Lorenz, emphasize that the emotions of birds are not so different from our own. Birds, for example, can exhibit behavior that is readily interpreted by us as curiosity, grief, affection, anger, and fear. It is not unthinkable that they respond in much the same way as we do to prickling sensations of the skin. They enjoy these sensations and go out of their way to bathe in substances that will produce the soothing or tingling effects that are so pleasurable.

The answer to the question of anting in birds seems much less complicated when viewed from the standpoint of the seasonal molting periods. However, the solution isn't this easy. We are confronted with the question of anting in cats and squirrels, which of course have no feathers but which shed their fur. They, too, may feel the need for a counterirritant. Then there is the question of instances of year-round anting in captive birds as reported by Roy Ivor in Canada and Lovie Whitaker in this country. Would wild birds ant through the year if they only had the ingredients? Unlike cage birds, which are supplied with ants by the experimenter, the wild bird has to find its own ant colonies, and this might not be so easy in northern temperate regions in winter. This question has been answered for North Carolina by Mrs. Potter, who tells me that in her latitude ants are active through the winter. She has no less than twelve active ant colonies in her yard during the winter months but has observed no anting at this time of the year by birds. Even captive birds, when supplied with all the ingredients they need, do not necessarily continue to ant

*House cat rolling in catnip*

through the colder months. Captive Pekin robins, for example, anted in hot weather but threw the ants out of their aviary in the winter.

Anting may sometimes be conducted solely for the sake of the exciting side effects. Cage birds, with little else to do, seem to ant for this reason. This would also apply to hand-reared or excessively tame birds that have learned how to ant with lighted cigarettes and other exotic substances. Completely wild birds, on the other hand, would almost certainly need a utilitarian reason for anting. They have little time for anything but limited self-indulgence; also they can't permit themselves forms of activity that overly interfere with their constant watch for enemies.

We seem to be a lot closer than we were even ten years ago to finding a solution to why birds ant. But I would caution against making sweeping generalizations. What one researcher may regard as the answer may soon be disputed by someone else, and perhaps in an altogether different part of the world. This is how progress in science is attained. No theory is unshakable until it has been tested over and over, and even well-established theories are sometimes overturned.

In spite of my feelings of caution, I strongly welcome the present emphasis upon molt in birds. I am persuaded that somewhere in this area lies the answer and not in older theories relating to external parasites. Nevertheless there is seldom a single reason that explains a behavior pattern. It would appear that birds ant to sooth skin irritation during the molt period and for pleasure motives. Even more reasons, including those given for anting, can be given for bathing in water. Reasons for dusting and sunning may be the same as those for anting. But we still can't be certain. Let's hope that before long others like Chisholm in Australia and Potter and Hauser in North Carolina will guide us still further in this most intriguing field of bird behavior.

# Eluding Enemies | 5

Those who do their bird-watching at home have an advantage over those who may cover many miles in the field without witnessing a single episode involving behavior, food habits, predation, or any other noteworthy events in the lives of birds. How then to enjoy two worlds, watching birds at home and tramping the countryside in the expectation of adding to one's knowledge of birdlife? Without realizing it, I took a course that resolved this question by becoming a bird lister when I went far afield and a behaviorist when I stayed at home. This has worked out very nicely over the years since I first became interested in birds. Since I enjoy hiking and being out-of-doors, I am not disappointed if it has been a poor day for the list. In fact, my lust for listing sated a number of years ago, I gave it up. Instead, I store away in my memory the sights, smells, and sensations I enjoy when I'm off by myself in the woods and far away from traffic and too many people. If I see a bird that is unusual to my area or that I haven't seen for a long time, that is just another of the joys of being close to nature.

At home I indulge in a very different kind of bird-watching. Since the birds are so much tamer and there are so many more of them in one place, all I have to do is look out the window and watch. I can get almost equally good results by sitting in a corner of the yard with notebook in hand. Not every day is there something different or worth recording. Even so I make a habit of jotting down seemingly insignificant details. Who knows what help a detail may give in solving a complicated problem in bird behavior? The importance of keeping careful notes that contain references to time, date, place, and weather conditions can scarcely be overemphasized.

Of course you can enjoy birds without going to this trouble. However, these days, when people rely so much more on opportunities close to home for the satisfactions of life, it pays to keep notes, a bird diary, or some other record that will help broaden one's interest and provide information that might be used for any one of several purposes later on.

### Sudden departures

Lacking song, beauty, and much else that we applaud in birds, the house sparrow, which first gained a foothold in North America in the early 1850s, does have a tenacity and will to live that can hardly be surpassed in the animal kingdom. One of the secrets of its success is never to be taken by surprise. Wherever it happens to be, it takes the precaution of suddenly flying off at frequent intervals whether or not it has been disturbed or alarmed. These sudden departures confuse other birds as well as ourselves. Birds quietly feeding with house sparrows also often take fright and fly away; they and we look for a cause without seeing one.

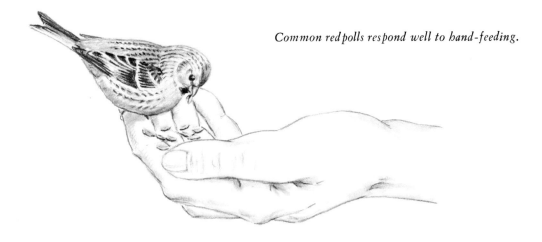

*Common redpolls respond well to hand-feeding.*

George Shiras III,* writing in the mid-1920s, calls the house sparrow the
most timorous of all birds. He noted that although the flock around his house
was never molested and never without access to feeders, there was always a
state of alarm. If someone so much as approached a closed window, the flock
at the bird feeder whirred away to a nearby treetop.

Like Shiras, I have found that house sparrows live lives dominated by fear.
Noise, motion, or nothing at all sends them fleeing from my bird feeders. The
birds never show the slightest confidence in me. I am as much a part of a hostile
world as a dog, cat, or swiftly diving small hawk. My generous food offerings
are not appreciated or acknowledged. I feel slighted; yet, at the same time, I
admire the pluck of this street urchin that has done so well where other birds
would fail.

I shouldn't imply that the house sparrow is the only bird that dashes off
before its meal is half finished. This is a common procedure among all feeding-
station visitors. Some leave abruptly, like the house sparrow; others pause a
moment before they depart; while still others wait out an alarm by crouching
where they are. Common redpolls that visited my feeders at Moose Hill in
Massachusetts one winter exhibited two types of behavior depending upon where
they happened to be. When feeding in a nearby weed field, they were just as
flighty and ill at ease as house sparrows. After feeding restlessly in one spot for
a brief time, the flock would fly off to another spot for an equally brief feeding
and then perhaps take refuge in the nearest treetop. These were rhythmical,
spontaneous movements unrelated to specific danger, unless it was danger from
the unseen that might attack without warning.

In more sheltered situations, such as the well-planted yard where my
feeders were located, the redpolls behaved altogether differently. The no longer
nervous flock would settle wherever food was present on the snow-covered
ground or to be had at bird feeders. If I sat quietly where the birds were feeding, sooner or later members of the flock would gather around me, and sometimes a few would take food from my hand. The difference between the redpoll
and the house sparrow is that the former had left the familiar dangers of the
wild behind and in civilization changed its behavior entirely. The much more

* George Shiras III, *Hunting Wild Life with Camera and Flashlight*, Vol. 2 (Washington, D.C.: National
Geographic Society, 1935).

domesticated house sparrow is aware of the unpredictableness of mankind and never lets itself be caught unawares near him. Only in the sanctuary of some city parks does it begin to let down its guard. Whether Hyde Park in London or Lafayette Square in Washington, the eager birds gather wherever food is being offered. Bolder birds even take food from the hand or alight on an arm or shoulder. The city park sparrow is an altogether different bird from the suburban or country sparrow. I was surprised when in a small New England town, house sparrows ensconced inside a privet hedge allowed me to approach within inches of them. The explanation was that they knew they were safe inside the hedge. Outside its network of twigs and branches, these sparrows would be the same nervous, flighty birds that one sees everywhere.

### Sentinels

Neither we nor birds, apparently, can place very much confidence in the so-called sentinels birds are said to post when the flock is feeding. Margaret M.

*Meadowlarks, which depend on protective coloration, usually stay put when danger threatens.*

Nice* points out that bird sentinels are not to be trusted. She states that there are many examples of the sentinels themselves deserting their posts without giving warning of danger to the rest of the flock. Crows are said to post sentinels, as well as a number of other birds, including the California quail.

It may be added that there also seems to be little evidence to support the contention that crows sometimes hold trials in which a member of the flock is either pardoned for committing some offense or is executed by its comrades. If such proceedings really take place, it would seem more likely that the flock is deliberating the fate of an injured, sick, or aged member that is not able to keep up with the others.

### Protective coloration

As a rule birds are much more nervous and flighty in the open than they are near cover. The extent of the nervousness depends upon the species. The well-camouflaged meadowlark spends most of its life in the open and reacts to danger by freezing wherever it happens to be. Its plumage blends so well with a grassy background that even a keen-eyed hawk is apt to be deceived. On the other hand, not all open-country birds blend so well with their surroundings. Some, like the belted kingfisher and male vermilion flycatcher, are conspicuous enough for all the world to see. How do these brightly colored birds avoid being preyed upon?

An answer of sorts has been supplied by a British investigator, H. B. Cott.† Although I am not completely convinced by his findings, he has presented good evidence to show that on the whole birds whose flesh is most edible are protectively colored, while those with poor-tasting flesh are brightly colored and also more likely to live in the open. Cott tested his theory by exposing bodies of dead birds, minus their feathers, and then watching to see how his tasters (cats and carrion-eating wasps) responded. Birds with the brightest plumage had the lowest palatability ratings.

* Margaret M. Nice, *Studies in the Life History of the Song Sparrow* (Trans. Linn. Society, New York, no. 4, 1937).
† H. B. Cott, *Proceedings of the Zoological Society of London* 116 (1946): 371–524.

Regardless of how unpleasing its flesh may taste, the brightly colored bird cannot expect to entirely escape the attention of predators. Some predators will have to learn by trial and error which birds taste well and which do not. Also some predators, including the domestic cat, kill for sport and do not necessarily eat their victims. David Lack,* writing of the British robin, tells of cats that continue to kill this bird even though its flesh makes them sick. On our side of the Atlantic, cats kill blue jays even though they do not always eat them. Presumably the blue jay, a brightly colored bird often in the open, isn't as tasty as many other birds that find a place on the house cat's menu.

Where I live in Maryland, the male cardinal is quite bold about coming out into the open and is usually the least disturbed of all birds when a small hawk puts in an appearance. The less colorful female generally stays well within denser stands of shrubbery. On one occasion in winter, when a sharp-shinned hawk was in the yard, a male cardinal was seen in the same lilac bush with the hawk. While I watched from a distance, the cardinal, more curious than afraid, flitted from branch to branch as though trying to get a better look at the hawk.

* David Lack, *The Life of the Robin* (London: H. F. & G. Witherby, 1965).

*A bird of the open, the belted kingfisher seems relatively immune to attacks by predators.*

Even though the two birds were at times no more than three or four feet apart, the small hawk finally flew away without having so much as made a feint in the cardinal's direction. Did the cardinal know it was safe and did the hawk know that the cardinal wasn't worth its effort? The episode revealed how little we really know about such matters.

## Alarms

Small woodland birds have the advantage of always having a sufficient amount of cover to hide in or dash behind. As a result, the woodland bird is not as flighty as its dull-colored neighbors that live in more open country. We see this at the feeding station. The small woodpeckers, chickadees, and nuthatches that spend their lives within the sheltering foliage of the woodland seldom dash away unless there is a genuine alarm. But the way visiting flocks of red-wings, grackles, or cowbirds fly off to cover and then quickly come back reminds one of the house sparrow. Sometimes the blackbirds follow the lead of house sparrows, sometimes they fly off on their own. Neither brightly colored nor inconspicuous, the darker-hued blackbirds, as well as starlings, seem to know they are vulnerable to predators.

Even more upsetting to birds than the alarms of house sparrows are the warning calls of blue jays and their realistic imitations of hawk calls. Self-appointed guardians, with a roguish nature that delights in teasing, blue jays and their western cousins never seem to tire of putting other birds to flight when there is no good reason. Nevertheless, many times their alarms are genuine. Blue jays, whatever their motives may be, take still other steps to look out for the safety of other birds. According to the somewhat overly anthropomorphic interpretation of a lady in New Jersey, at the first hint of a cat, blue jays fly to her window calling for help. On several occasions she saw jays fly into feeding flocks of small birds in order to herd them to safety. Blue jays in a Florida yard were reported to announce the presence of snakes. There were two occasions when the jays gave warning of the approach of a rattlesnake.

Jays, of course, are not the only birds that have sharp eyes and watch closely for any hint of danger. Every bird in the yard or at the feeder is involved to some degree in looking out for its own safety and consequently that of its companions. When watching birds at the feeder or birdbath, the observer will note that every time a bird lifts its head, it looks around ever so briefly before resuming its activity. Some individuals are more alert than others, and these will be the ones most likely to give the alarm. The flock, as a whole, will benefit, and this is as good a reason as any why birds find safety in numbers.

The alarm call, when it is sounded, will be readily recognized by other birds and the flock, regardless of its makeup, will quickly respond. Differences in tone or different notes will be used to announce specific enemies or degrees of danger. If a small bird hawk appears, a bird must not give away its presence; therefore it uses a high-pitched call that seems to come from nowhere in particular. Ground marauders, as a rule, give birds more time and once discovered are regarded as less dangerous. Birds react by giving different alarm calls than they would for a hawk, and their method is now to keep the marauder in view and sometimes to try to drive it away. Song sparrows give high-pitched "tik" notes to warn of a flying predator, but down-to-earth "tchunk" calls when the marauder is afoot or if cowbirds invade their territories. Similarly, chipping sparrows sound a "zeee" alarm if it is a hawk, a "chip" for a cat or squirrel. The house sparrow sounds a "kewkew" call when alarmed by people or cats and a "kruu" call if it is a hawk.

Depending upon the source of danger, there is either mass departure from the feeding area by every bird or a partial exodus that involves only more exposed birds. As a rule, birds at hanging or raised feeders feel more secure than birds on the ground and therefore are apt to be slower in departing. Grayish or brownish birds, relying upon their protective coloration, frequently stay where they are. On one occasion, a junco, its gray plumage blending closely with the ground, stayed on and continued feeding, when all the other birds left my feeders. Mourning doves also tend to stay where they are, but, with these frequently overstuffed birds, laziness may be a factor.

Many of the duller-plumaged birds seem aware of their advantage and resort to a ruse known as freezing. This means they stay rigidly motionless wherever they happen to be and sometimes long after danger has passed. Nearly all small woodland birds that frequent trunks and limbs of trees employ this ruse, and so do duller-colored ground-feeding birds. The technique seems made

for slow-flying birds like woodpeckers, nuthatches, titmice, and creepers. I have
seen a downy woodpecker waiting out an alert with its bill poised for the next
attack upon a piece of suet. As soon as the reassuring note of a chickadee told
that the coast was clear, the bill descended and feeding resumed as though
nothing had happened. Aretas A. Saunders* tells of two brown creepers that
were engaged in a fight over rights to a suet basket. After an alarm sounded,
the birds remained frozen without visible movement for fourteen minutes. At
the end of this time, with the danger over, they went right back to fighting
again.

A cat minding its own business and walking leisurely across the lawn is
likely to be ignored, and so are romping dogs or playing children. These are
distractions that may cause birds to keep their distance but otherwise do not
interfere with normal activities. On the other hand, if a cat, by its stealthy
movements, labels itself a hunter, birds follow its every step and by their cries
announce to the whole world that danger is at hand. Blue jays are particularly

* Aretas A. Saunders, *The Lives of Wild Birds* (Garden City, N.Y.: Doubleday & Co., Inc., 1954).

*A marauding cat may be in for trouble
if a blue jay is near.*

vociferous in announcing the presence of a marauding cat or any suspicious prowler. Their tactics range from tweaking a cat by the tail to ganging up and driving off any enemy that they are a match for. If the enemy is too powerful, they relieve their emotions by resorting to clamorous vocal demonstrations.

When birds freeze, they also keep silent. They instinctively know that sound can give their presence away just as surely as movement. This is why the writer who says "the woods became silent as the hunter steathily approached his quarry" is largely correct in his description. Although jays may give their warning calls, other birds are likely to fall silent when their suspicions are aroused.

I am always struck by the way woodpeckers so often discontinue their loud tapping in trees when I'm trying to get a better look at them. Although I am armed only with binoculars, they mistrust my motives and become silent. On one occasion, the woodpecker that had been doing the tapping turned out to be a flicker. When I finally focused my binoculars on the bird, it was going through

*Blue jays are both the friends and foes
of other birds.*

all the motions of pecking against a dead branch but was making no noise. Are woodpeckers able to continue their work silently when they become aware of a possible enemy? This is something I plan to look into more thoroughly.

### False alarms

Both eastern and western jays are equally gifted when it comes to clearing the feeding station by sounding false alarms. This is a ruse that usually clears out the competition and gives jays free access to the food. Using either its own harsh alarm call or imitated screams of red-tailed or red-shouldered hawks, the blue jay arrives with such a flourish that the feeding station is immediately abandoned. It is the same effect exactly as if a real hawk appeared. But if the same tactic is used over and over by the jays, other birds catch on and ignore the raucous demonstrations. At my Moose Hill bird feeders the jays had overworked their stratagem. On the other hand, at my Maryland bird feeders, jay alarms are usually in earnest and even the chickens scurry for cover. In South Carolina jays heeded their own alarm calls and disappeared along with the rest of the birds. The role of jays as sentinels was especially apparent at my Virginia bird feeders. When jays were around, there was an alarm on an average of about one every ten minutes. With no jays, the alarms dropped to approximately one every hour.

There can be no doubt that jays exert an influence on the bird community far beyond their numbers. Their alarm notes both save lives and cause confusion. This is true not only at the feeding station but also in the wild. Many a deer, wild turkey, ruffed grouse, or pheasant has had its life saved by the warning cries of jays. In the West, game animals have Steller's and scrub jays to thank. As soon as a hunter with his gun enters the woods, the jays seem to know it and begin alerting whatever game may be in the vicinity. In much the same way jays notify other birds and ourselves if they are suspicious about any visitor to our yard. Jays not only keep a predator in view but often attempt to drive it away. Blue jays at times are willing to tackle a shrike or sharp-shinned hawk but not the larger, more powerful Cooper's hawk. These services by jays are appreciated by feeding-station operators, who take a dim view of birds being snatched away by predators of any kind.

While some of its actions unintentionally assist other birds and save lives, the blue jay after all looks out for itself. We cannot overlook the fact that the blue jay at times turns predator and takes the eggs and young of other birds. These depredations are usually on a small scale, and probably cease altogether if the blue jay has access at bird feeders to adequate supplies of foods that contain calcium and protein. However true this may be, the bird has a glint in its eye that isn't to be trusted by other birds. Without warning, a blue jay may suddenly attack and kill another bird feeding alongside it at the bird feeder. Rare cases of this involve a downy woodpecker, pine siskin, purple finch, and dark-eyed junco, each at widely separated feeding stations.

The false alarm, a jay trademark, is sometimes used by other birds and for much the same reasons. G. E. Smith, writing in *Audubon* for September–October 1956, states that crows, cousins of jays, near his feeder in British Columbia gave warning calls which frightened small birds at his feeder. He suspected that the crows did this for sport. The English blackbird, a thrush not to be confused with our red-winged blackbird, is known to sound a false alarm when maneuvering for handouts at city park benches. It rushes in to feed during the brief interval that larger birds are "taken in." Reports have it that another British bird, the blue titmouse, employs false alarms for "mischievous purposes."

### Mobbing

By its nature the bird-feeding station is a lively, sometimes quarrelsome place, where one may get the impression that it is every bird for itself. But, in spite of outward appearances, there is a surprising amount of community spirit that transcends the occasional fights and bickering. Birds, as we have seen, warn each other of enemies through an easily understood, universal language. Also at times birds help each other in ways that seem selfless even by our standards. Evening grosbeaks at a Quebec feeding station treated an injured comrade as an outcast, but a "tender-hearted" male began taking care of the injured bird and saw to it that this bird had its turn at the feeder during slack periods. Another example of this kind was reported by the New England ornithologist Edward Howe Forbush. He tells of an old, worn, partially blind blue jay that was fed and guarded by its companions.

Equally suggestive of a bond of brotherhood is the communal rite known as mobbing, wherein birds join together to thwart a common enemy. As defined by the British ornithologist, P. H. T. Hartley, mobbing is a demonstration made by a bird against a potential or supposed enemy belonging to another and more powerful species. It is initiated by a member of the weaker species and is not a reaction to an attack upon this species. I might add that mobbing is conducted by more than one bird and that frequently every bird within sight and hearing joins in. From the smallest wrens to blustering jays, birds gather from all sides to deliver the strongest protest they are capable of. Amid a din of calls and chatterings, the frenzied birds, some flying, some moving from perch to perch, feign attacks and sometimes threaten an eye or other vulnerable part with their bills. Although birds have been known to kill snakes in mobbing attacks, usually these demonstrations are completely sham. The predator, perhaps ruffled, escapes with harm only to its dignity. After letting off steam and letting the predator know that it has been spotted and can no longer take its prey by surprise, the mobbing throng, having accomplished its mission, disperses.

That mobbing is an effective way to subdue a predator is obvious from the way the tables are turned. The cat or hawk that has been frustrated in its designs will, as likely as not, leave the scene. Birds can then resume feeding or whatever else they were doing. However, there is a strange side to mobbing. Most such attacks are directed against owls, which for the most part do their feeding at night. One can get the impression that birds are getting back at an ancient enemy that is at a disadvantage in bright daylight. Whether this is true or not, most owls can see well enough during the day and some, including the short-eared, hawk, snowy, and pygmy, hunt by day. Therefore, whatever the time of day, small birds are subjecting themselves to a certain amount of risk when they take on an owl. Under the cover of darkness owls are implacable enemies, some species more than others. Arthur A. Allen, in a 1924 issue of *The Auk,* reported, on the basis of remains of victims, that a single pair of screech owls near his Ithaca, New York, home captured at least ninety-four individual birds of twenty-four species to feed their young. So in a very large sense the daytime mobbing of owls would seem to be a way that birds settle old scores.

Birds tend to pick on the species of owl that give them the most trouble while leaving less dangerous owls alone. Crows, inveterate owl mobbers, vent their wrath chiefly on great horned and barred owls; blue jays, on the other hand, as well as most small woodland birds, single out the screech owl for special attention. In the West, the six-inch-long pygmy owl is such a menace that the woodland bird community becomes alive with flashing wings and angry calls when one is discovered. The day-flying short-eared owl, in my experience, is not mobbed. Whether this is because it is diurnal in its habits or rarely given to attacking small birds, I am not sure. I am speaking of this owl on Nantucket, where it is not uncommonly seen gliding ghostlike over moorland covered with patches of fog.

Blue jays, which delight in having an advantage over a foe, are often the first to spot an owl and the last to desist in venting abuse. Jays, like other birds, locate owls chiefly by seeing them. But, as any bird-watcher knows, all one has to do is to give a good imitation of a screech owl (which incidentally does not screech) and birds will begin appearing from all over the place.

Crows sometimes exceed the jays in vehemence by pursuing the owl for long distances if they have been able to goad it into taking flight. A large flock of crows, cawing madly and making passes at an invisible enemy somewhere in the depth of a conifer grove, will almost certainly have discovered an owl. This, again, is a fact well known to bird-watchers and an aid to finding one of the larger owls. Owls hate crows, crows hate owls; therefore when these adversaries meet in the forest they leave little doubt of that.

In well-populated districts, cats seem to come under mobbing attacks more than any other predator. I have observed that not every cat is singled out for this treatment, only cats that through their actions betray an interest in dining on freshly killed bird. A cat that used to take its noon siesta on my bird feeder was exempt from any disturbance. Birds knew it was up to no harm. On the other hand, a cat prowling in shrubbery near the bird feeder or climbing a tree during the nesting season is almost certain to attract a throng of birds. A black cat in a tree in my Massachusetts yard attracted first the attention of blue jays, and then grackles, robins, and smaller birds. After putting on a noisy demonstration, the mobbing throng drifted away, apparently bored by the cat's inactivity and ready to get on with other business. The cat, no worse for the experience, then came down the tree.

The fine distinction between dangerous versus harmless individuals that applies to owls and cats applies equally well to hawks. Frances Hamerstrom, in an article in a 1957 issue of *The Condor,* observed that his tame red-tailed hawk was mobbed only about half as many times when it was well fed as when it was hungry. Birds apparently recognize a hungry hawk by the flattened appearance of the top of the head, the erect feathers on the hind neck, the slightly erect wings, and the more upright position of the body. Knowing that this is a bird that may attack at any moment, possible prey species are much more apt to gather for a mobbing attack. On the other hand, the hawk that does not inspire fear may be treated with complete indifference. Many times I have seen small birds perched on the same wires with a kestrel, or even more daring, feeding unconcernedly near one of the accipiters. On one occasion in Florida, two brown-headed nuthatches were searching for food on the limb of a pine tree on which sat a Cooper's hawk. As I watched to see what might happen as the nuthatches

*Most mobbing attacks by small birds are directed against owls. These birds are pursuing a screech owl.*

approached to within a few feet of their foe, the hawk took wing and flew away. The situation was no different from that mentioned earlier involving the male cardinal and the sharp-shinned hawk. Sharp-shins, as I know from long experience, visit my yard for only one purpose—to make a meal out of one of my bird guests. The nuthatches may have sized up the hawk near them and consequently knew from its manner that they had nothing to fear.

But good visibility is needed if a bird is to recognize the outline of a small hawk as it flies over. On or near the ground a bird cannot see through obstructing foliage or overhead branches. At the same time, the winged predator, high overhead, cannot see potential prey through such barriers. This is why the well-planted yard, especially one that contains evergreens, is such a safe refuge compared to the more open yard. Still, there is always one ever-present fear. This is the fear of the small, swift-flying hawk, regardless of cover conditions, that will suddenly dive through the foliage to snatch any bird that hasn't been quick enough to get out of its path.

As we have seen, birds have no trouble recognizing owls and seem perceptive enough to distinguish well-fed hawks from hungry ones. They also know how

*A red-shouldered hawk poised to make an attack*

to tell dangerous species of hawks from ones that are relatively harmless. According to Niko Tinbergen, the German behaviorist,* young birds can recognize an accipiter, when it flies over, by its long-tailed, stubby-winged, drawn-in neck appearance. This he proved by pulling a model attached to a wire over enclosures containing young waterfowl or young gallinaceous birds. When the model appeared overhead, the young birds, even though they had never been exposed to a winged predator, ran for cover. But when the model was reversed so that the tail came first, the young birds showed no alarm. The model now looked like a crane or goose in flight. These experiments helped show that recognizing dangerous hawks is an inborn ability in birds.

Although birds can recognize hawks in flight by their tail and wing patterns, they are like us in needing time and proper visibility in order to make accurate identifications. When unsure, which is most of the time, they dash for cover, or, in some more aggressive species, fly out in pursuit of whatever it is that is flying over. Brewer's blackbirds, as reported in Bent's *Life Histories,* can become alarmed when a crow, large hawk, night heron, or gull flies over. Even a plane passing over can upset them. Whether deceived or simply because of extra aggressiveness, an eastern kingbird, as reported in a 1935 issue of *The Auk,* took wing to attack boldly a slow, low-flying biplane. Kingbirds sally forth to harass almost anything that flies, so this pursuit of a small plane by one of these birds wasn't too surprising. A chickadee at my Virginia feeding station, taking alarm when a lazily soaring turkey vulture appeared overhead, may simply have needed a lesson in identification!

But the small birds that mobbed a chuck-will's-widow knew what they were doing. The episode, as reported in a 1967 issue of *The Auk,* could easily have been interpreted as an example of mistaken identity. The chuck-will is a big-headed, large-eyed nocturnal bird that could easily be mistaken for an owl. Although dominantly an insect-eater, catching flying insects as it zooms through the night skies, the chuck-will is also known to pursue and capture small birds. Thus the birds involved in the mobbing attack had doubtless recognized a true enemy.

* Niko Tinbergen, *Animal Behavior* (Alexandria, Va.: Life Nature Library, 1965).

*Part-time predators*

The indifference birds show when a famished or crippled large hawk begins eating suet and other tidbits at a feeding station is an example of how quickly birds can change their attitudes from fear to acceptance. The once-dangerous hawk has suddenly become innocuous, and when this happens birds seem to know it immediately. They are equally astute in sizing up *Homo sapiens,* their most equivocal foe, who sometimes appears with a gun and other times with food. Birds, in their busy lives, haven't time to take exception to every creature that may at some time have turned on them. Finding food and rearing families is taxing enough without having to join in a mobbing performance or dash into bushes every time an old enemy appears on the scene. Therefore they strike a compromise, maintaining extra vigilance when it comes to implacable foes and relaxing to some degree when the enemy seems easier to get along with.

The almost uncanny way that waterfowl stay beyond gun range and even know the difference between live birds and decoys is a subject that forever tantalizes hunters. The same acute birds that have braved shotgun blasts settle down in winter to a complacent existence on city-park lakes or wherever else they are protected. But there is a certain tenseness, an air of watching, that separates a truly wild bird from semidomesticated residents. The native North American turkey, one of the wariest of game birds, knows where it is safe and under exactly what conditions it can trust man. At the Welder Wildlife Refuge near Sinton, Texas, I threw a handful of grain toward a flock of turkeys fully expecting the birds to fly off in alarm. Instead the flock advanced toward me with as much confidence as domestic fowl. Driving South Texas highways early in the morning, I sometimes saw flocks of turkeys along the road's edge. These truly wild birds would have disappeared in an instant at the sight of a man on foot. However, they recognized speeding vehicles as harmless. Members of the crow family have learned that it is safe to feed along roadsides. The once heavily persecuted common crow is now making itself at home in towns and cities, and sometimes shows itself at bird feeders. The ring-necked pheasants and quail that visit feeding stations are additional proof that, as man changes his ways and becomes less dangerous, birds lose no time in accepting that fact.

Birds have a harder time deciding when the enemy is dressed in feathers and behaves almost like any other member of the feeding flock. Not so different in appearance from the mockingbird but with a black mask and more contrastingly black and white plumage, the loggerhead shrike presents birds with one of their most difficult identification problems. This was true at my Florida feeding station near Gainesville. Almost any hour of the day through the fall and early winter, I could look out and see a loggerhead shrike perched on a pole or wire somewhere nearby. Immobile and ignored by other birds, the shrike looked the picture of tranquil indifference. Its only show of purpose was now and then to fly to the ground, seize a grasshopper or mouse, and carry it off in its hooked bill. Shrikes are known for their habit of impaling excess food on a thorn or barb of a wire fence. My bird was no different from any other butcher bird, as shrikes are sometimes called, and with the first cool weather in January this bird began to reveal another side to its nature. First I saw it in hot pursuit of a brown thrasher, and later in the day, when I visited my ground banding traps in a nearby pecan grove, I found one of my traps holding a dead white-throated sparrow, a terrified cardinal, and a wildly flapping loggerhead shrike. After releasing the shrike, which was obviously to blame for the damage, I picked up the cardinal, but it was too late. The bird expired in my hand, having died of fright. A few days

*Loggerhead shrikes commonly impale their prey on barbs of wire fences or thorns of plants.*

later I saw a small flock of cedar waxwings whirl past me in a panic. Apparently a mockingbird, flying into the same bush where they were feeding, looked much too much like a shrike, and hence the precipitous departure. Normally birds do not show fear of a mockingbird in spite of its sometimes aggressive habits. With cooler weather, loggerhead shrikes often begin turning to small birds as an extra source of protein. Roy Ivor,* speaking of the larger northern shrike, which is more of a bird killer, states that birds do not instinctively know it as an enemy. Not until birds have been exposed to danger a few times from this source do they begin to recognize shrikes as enemies.

The bird that drops its egg into some other bird's nest, leaving incubation and all parental duties to foster parents, is rarely regarded as an enemy. Certainly the brown-headed cowbird is not molested or singled out for any special attention when it visits the yard or feeding station. Cowbirds tend to be clannish, staying in tight flocks made up of their own kind or traveling sometimes with other members of the blackbird family. Small birds whose nests are parasitized sometimes catch on to what is taking place and take appropriate measures. Song sparrows, according to Margaret Nice, are on to the cowbird and attempt to drive this intruder away when it approaches their nests. The yellow warbler generally builds another nest over the one that has received a cowbird egg. A six-storied yellow warbler nest was found in Michigan that contained in its various layers no less than eleven cowbird eggs.

Surprising tolerance is shown by most birds toward crows, magpies, jays, and grackles, which are nest robbers in season and relatively trustworthy at other times of the year. Birds also fail to harbor grudges against squirrels and chipmunks, which are nest robbers. They eat as calmly alongside these messmates as they do when only birds are present. Sometimes their confidence is misplaced.

A gray squirrel at my Moose Hill feeder made a sudden lunge at an evening grosbeak but missed. At a neighbor's feeder, a gray squirrel pounced upon and killed a chickadee. Since the dead chickadee was not carried off or eaten, my neighbor thought this killing might have been an accident. Minor depredations, such as these, by gray squirrels are nothing compared to more serious problems at bird feeders from red squirrels. The smaller red squirrel has more of an

---

* Roy Ivor, *I Live with Birds* (Chicago: Follett, 1968).

appetite for small birds. A number of reports of its predatory activities at feeders
have come to me from Canadian correspondents. Also it is more of a nest robber
than the gray squirrel. Even the little chipmunk, which looks so innocent, is
not to be trusted. When at Moose Hill, a lady brought me a fledgling blue jay
whose head had received an injury from a chipmunk. And John K. Terres, in
his book *The Wonders I See,** tells of a chipmunk at the New York Zoological
Gardens that dashed out from the shrubbery, seized a house sparrow, and then
carried it off.

When one stops to think of it, predation at bird feeders, including the
inroads of small hawks and cats, is rarely a matter of any consequence. I seldom
see more than one bird a year killed at any of the many bird feeders I have
managed. Perhaps another ten birds are killed that I do not see—losses that are
barely enough to weed out aged, crippled, and diseased birds. Concerted action
by members of the flock is the reason that losses, as a rule, are so negligible.
Alarm calls, mobbing actions, and alertness to predators are effective ways that
birds protect themselves. Also they know enough to stay away should a dangerous predator take up residence in the immediate vicinity of a feeder.

The heaviest losses from predation occur during the period when the nest
is occupied and immediately afterward. In spite of all the precautions birds take
to put their nests in secure places, a large percentage are discovered and robbed.
An equally dangerous period is at hand when the young, first out of the nest,
are unable to fly well and are not yet on to the ways of the world. D. Summers-
Smith, in his book, *The House Sparrow,* † states that about half the young sparrows that leave the nest die in the first month that they are on their own.

Birds have a better perception than we do concerning predation. They waste
no time reacting to squirrels and other part-time predators that may never turn
on them. Rather they reserve their energies for the predators they fear most. It
is the small hawk coming upon them from out of nowhere or movements in the
grass betraying a four-legged predator that stir them into action. With a little
help from us in the way of evergreen plantings and other dense growth, birds
at our feeders are fully capable of looking out for themselves.

---

* John K. Terres, *The Wonders I See* (New York: J. B. Lippincott Co., 1960).
† D. Summers-Smith, *The House Sparrow* (London: Collins, 1963).

*Enormous flocks of passenger pigeons filled the skies of this country until about 1870.*

# Confrontations | 6

The expression "birds of a feather flock together" is as apt as any of the old folk sayings. One of the things that impresses us most about birds is their sociability. Over much of the year, birds of many species join with others of their kind to form flocks. The flock may be a small one, made up of a few individuals, or so large that the sky is blackened when the flock passes over. One of the most awe-inspiring sights of early America was the huge flocks of passenger pigeons that literally blotted out the sun. Today, now that the passenger pigeon is gone, we must be content with the enormous flocks of grackles, red-wings, and other assorted blackbirds that stretch across the sky for miles when going to or from the roost.

Whether large or small, the flock is a smoothly functioning unit that knows where it is going and what it is doing without any conspicuous direction. This is unlike human societies, where there is always a form of leadership as well as a form of dissent. How members of a flock decide which foraging area they are going to when they leave the roost in the morning is one of those difficult questions that has so far been unanswered. All we know is that a flock of red-winged blackbirds, when it streams out from its roost in the morning, goes directly to its destination. There are no signs of friction or debate among the members. Once in the field, the birds spread out among the stubble, each individual feeding close to its comrades and the entire flock moving in the same direction.

When woodpeckers, titmice, nuthatches, and other small birds appear in mixed flocks in the fall, we are likely to witness the same kind of purpose and discipline that governs the red-wing flock. This will be true in spite of differences in feeding habits. The benefits of alarm calls sounded by alert members and of many eyes versus fewer for food finding outweigh any disadvantages. There could also be another motive. Birds seem to enjoy one another's company.

Through the day mixed flocks of woodland birds travel widely in search of food. When a flock appears at a feeding station, there will be a spell of intense activity, some birds coming to suet or suet mixes, others to sunflower, and others to mixed seed and grain. Each species picks the food and feeding places that best suit its needs. The flock eats without undue friction, and then, as though responding to a common impulse, departs. Anyone observing such a flock will be correct if he assumes that the chickadees are the leaders. These inquisitive birds do seem to have definite notions about where they will look for food.

As the day progresses, some members will drop out along the way until finally only the chickadees are left to seek out roosting places in dense stands of evergreens. The following day will be much the same, with other birds attaching themselves to the chickadee flock and many of the same places revisited.

The sociability and general lack of discord within the flock is not severely taxed when birds find insufficient food. They eat whatever there is and move on. This is as true in the wild as it generally is at the feeding station. The secret of nonviolent behavior among birds lies in their acceptance of a social hierarchy that allows some birds to have superior privileges over others. Not all birds, as we shall see, abide by the rules. But there is enough compliance to prevent chaotic disorder.

### Food without fighting

To learn the rules of conduct that govern birds, it helps to watch a flock of chickens. After initial fights, in which members find their place in what is known as a "pecking order," the birds settle down to relatively peaceful coexistence. Winners tend to stay winners and losers stay losers. A defeated bird soon knows enough to stay out of the way of its superiors. Not to do so will likely lead to a sharp peck. If a subordinate bird should revolt, it will have little chance of success. It has lost so many times before that it does not have the spirit to put up a proper fight.

The type of relationship just described will prevail throughout the flock. There will be a top-ranking individual (rooster or hen) that can peck any other member of the flock with impunity, a second-ranking bird that can peck any but the top bird, and so on down until the lowest individual is reached. This unenviable bird is pecked by every member of the flock and cannot return the pecks. Among domestic fowl to be henpecked is literally the true state of affairs for most members of the flock.

Wild birds are not as restricted in their social relationships as their distant kin in the barnyard. The pecking order found in domestic poultry depends upon each bird's knowing its own and every other bird's status. Forgetfulness in poultry is rewarded by a well-placed peck. If the farmer should purchase more chickens and place them in among the others, there would be frightful disorder for a few days, with the new arrivals getting the worst of it. Eventually the newcomers would become integrated, with each finding a place that might be near the bottom of the pecking order.

*House sparrow in full pursuit of a pigeon*

Birds living in the wild frequently establish well-knit pecking-order relationships where the flock is not too large. But these relationships, as determined in chickadees, juncos, and tree sparrows, are reasonably flexible. A bird may be dominant under some conditions and some times of the year and not others. Much depends upon where the bird is. Like a dog defending its master's yard, the bird is a great deal more determined on its home territory. Defending a mate, nest site, special food supply, or place at a roost brings forth the required amount of spirit to win out over most rivals. Under these circumstances the bird is said to have "peck dominance."

Birds belonging to large flocks, and especially flocks whose composition is subject to frequent change, can hardly be expected to know their own status in a pecking order or that of very many other birds. Uncertainties regarding status may be a factor in the frequent bickering and sometimes all-out fights that occur in large flocks of starlings, evening grosbeaks, and purple finches.

Although wild birds have a harder time recognizing their places in a flock than domestic fowl, there is usually enough of a pecking order to ensure relatively peaceful relationships. Such fighting as does occur is chiefly between members of the same species. Anyone playing host to the winter finches will notice that perhaps nine out of ten "quarrels" are within the flock and do not involve outsiders. The quarrels seem to stem from one bird's getting into the way of another. The two birds involved at first try to settle their differences through sham fighting. The birds face each other in a crouching position, heads tilted forward and beaks partly open. One or both wings may be raised. The exact display differs from species to species. The message is always the same: "Get out of my way or else!" Usually one of the birds will back down. It either flies off or moves a few inches away. The ease with which differences are usually settled is part of a training that begins soon after young leave the nest. The young bird learns that it must accept a position commensurate with its size, sex, and physical prowess. To overstep its bounds means a quick reprisal.

Arthur A. Allen* observed that young common grackles coming to his feeding station were constantly fighting among themselves. He concluded that the birds were settling their status ratings in the pecking order. After each had

* Arthur A. Allen, *The Book of Birdlife* (Princeton, N.J.: D. Van Nostrand, 1960).

found its place, the fighting subsided. Disputes were now settled by elaborate displays that took the place of fighting. Adversaries would throw out their chests and point their bills skyward, at the same time often puffing out their feathers and raising their wings. The display over, the birds would go back to eating again.

The autocratic male cardinal that won't let his mate eat with him during the winter suddenly becomes very solicitous when the mating season approaches. Now his spouse eats with him and receives choice tidbits that he offers her while she appreciatively squats and flutters her wings. She now has the same status that he does in the flock. If he is a dominant bird, she is too. In birds, as well as people, there is such a thing as "marrying" to achieve social status.

Although the female may gain higher rank within the flock, she rarely has equal rights with her mate. This is seen not only in cardinals but in most species that visit feeding stations. A striking example, involving a pair of white-breasted nuthatches, was cited by William Brewster in *October Farm*.* The male in this pair, firmly in control of the suet feeder, would carefully give his mate small pieces of suet, which she would carry off to hide. But if she so much as dared

* William Brewster, *October Farm* (Cambridge, Mass.: Harvard University Press, 1936).

*Common grackles work off their hostility by going through a series of elaborate threat performances.*

gather suet herself at the feeder, she would be viciously driven off by her mate, who now regarded her as an interloper.

Birds visiting a feeding station for the first time may either accept a lower status or try to intimidate older residents. Sometimes sheer aggression works. With its appetite sharpened by hunger, the newcomer may possess a recklessness that will overcome its rivals. This seemed to be the case with the female robin that dominated my Florida feeder for a period in February. At first she chased every other bird, including a mockingbird. After four days, she neglected to chase a female cardinal. After a week, she was feeding peacefully with at least four other species, and a few days later she herself was chased by a red-bellied woodpecker and then a blue jay.

When birds of different species are thrown together for any length of time, it might be expected that friction would develop. This will not necessarily be the case at bird feeders if a variety of foods is offered and there are sufficient numbers and kinds of feeding devices. Customers will go to whatever foods and

feeders suit them best. Some will feed higher, some lower, and some will time
their visits in such a way as not to coincide with the busiest periods of feeding
activity. This is roughly parallel to the way birds sort themselves out in the
wild. Each species has its preferred foods and feeding niches. So, although many
times birds do feed in close associations with one another, such as happens in
the chickadee bands I have mentioned, there is seldom a problem from competition. The feeding activities of one species often help another by making a
difficult-to-obtain food more available. A good example in the wild is the breaking apart of rotting wood by woodpeckers. After a pileated woodpeacker had
been pounding on a fallen rotten log in a wooded tract in Florida, I saw a house
wren step out of the foliage and begin examining the log for the many insects
that had been uncovered. At bird feeders, stronger-billed birds demolish the
suet or more proficiently open sunflower seeds. These activities always result in
small particles of food falling on the bird feeder or dropping to the ground.
The weaker-billed birds gladly pick up the residue.

*A house wren moves in to feed on a log as soon as*
*a pileated woodpecker makes its*
*departure.*

When many birds are attracted to the same food, friction can develop. I've seen this happen particularly at feeding stations where a single food item is offered in a confined area. I recall that at one of my own feeders, chipping sparrows fed peacefully with each other when food was scattered widely on open ground. But when the birds were required to eat in a more confined space below a window, fighting broke out. Much of the belligerence seen in purple finches and evening grosbeaks is a result of crowding. This kind of problem can be greatly eased by spreading food out more widely. Some can be offered in small hanging feeders, some on bird tables, and some on the ground.

Even in the wild there are occasions when crowding occurs or when birds aggressively compete for the same food. This should make us feel better about the problems we sometimes unintentionally create. A pair of wood pewees I saw trying to chase off redstarts and other warblers were apparently guarding a swarm of flying insects they were feeding upon. Lawrence Kilham, in a note in a 1961 issue of *The Auk,* tells of the very possessive behavior of yellow-rumped warblers when guarding wild foods in winter. The small birds dart out and give chase to any other birds coming near, including much larger ones. The lengths that mockingbirds will go to in order to protect their winter supplies of small fruits know no bounds.

At the feeding station, larger, more aggressive birds usually take a domineering role, while smaller birds are more likely to have to wait their turn. Sometimes the tables are turned when, through sheer daring, smaller birds get the better of larger ones. If fighting takes place, it is usually at times when the composition of the feeding-station flock is undergoing its greatest change. The arrival of northern finches or spring migrants sometimes puts a strain on tempers. After a settling-in period, in which birds find a place for themselves in a loose hierarchy comprising dominant and subordinate species as well as the dominance relationships within a species, fighting becomes less frequent. It is replaced by mock fighting and displays which relieve tensions and remind individuals of their place in the pecking order. These performances do not always settle every dispute, however. Some, as we shall see, have a basis in deep-seated antagonisms that are hard to account for.

We see a lessening in the number of disputes at our bird feeders during very bad weather. Winifred S. Sabine, in a 1956 issue of *The Condor,* tells how the home junco flock, during a long period of heavy snow in Seattle, allowed juncos from the outside to feed with them. The same birds would have been chased away during more moderate weather. A blizzard in Iowa permitted a bird-bander, M. L. Jones, to catch a record forty-five downy woodpeckers, five hairy woodpeckers, and sixteen white-breasted nuthatches near his house in one day! Totals such as these, as I know from banding the same species at my bird feeders, would be unheard of under more normal conditions. When I was banding birds at my home in Virginia, a five-inch snow in January resulted in 3.26 times as many birds entering my traps as during a similar time period in mild weather. I attributed my increased take both to appetites whetted by the cold and a breakdown in territorial defense with consequently far fewer disputes.

### Vicious attacks

Rising straight up in the air, bill to bill and wings flapping wildly, birds remind us now and then of a more violent side to their dispositions. Some of the most violent fights involve the smallest birds. The four-and-a-half-inch-long male painted bunting sometimes kills another painted bunting in a fight over terri-

*Bill-to-bill and straight up into the air go two purple finches in "an argument" over priority.*

tory. The ill-tempered buntings also quarrel frequently at feeding stations with a number of the birds participating. Alexander Sprunt, Jr., describing the aggressive behavior of these brilliantly colored birds in Bent's *Life Histories,* states that the contestants sometimes become so absorbed in their battles that a passerby can easily pick one or two of the birds up in his hand.

The birdbander is well aware of the powers of a bird's beak or claws. If not careful, he may receive a painful wound when handling certain species. The hawks, with their hooked beaks and sharp talons, require the most care. But a turkey vulture I was attempting to corral struck out with its bill and left my hand bleeding. I've also received painful wounds when handling evening grosbeaks and cardinals. Both have a habit of seizing a finger in a viselike grip with their powerful beaks and refusing to let go. It doesn't take much imagination to realize how devastating birds can be when engaged in serious fighting with each other. This may explain the lengths they go to in order to avoid fighting.

When a battle is necessary, it can be a long rough-and-tumble affair reminiscent of the kind of fights between hero and villain seen on TV or in western movies. D. Summers-Smith, in his book on the house sparrow, tells of a battle between two female house sparrows that lasted for about an hour. The

fight, which began in a house gutter, spilled over onto a garage roof and the
ground. The birds became separated long enough to fly back to the gutter and
there again resumed the contest. Summers-Smith states that in house sparrows
males only attack males and females only females.

I have seen similar house sparrow encounters myself. Like painted buntings,
the contestants become so embroiled that it is sometimes possible to pick them
up. In one encounter, described by a friend, the victor maneuvered its rival
into a vulnerable position and delivered a death-dealing blow at the rear of
the skull. This occurred while an appreciative audience of other house sparrows
gathered around to watch. There is a reported case of a male killing another
male and eating its brains.

Starlings are not so different from house sparrows in their relationships
with each other and other birds. They love to fight and have many pet peeves.
They engage in the same kind of "street brawls" as house sparrows. Bitter engage-
ments between two starlings may go on and on. Other starlings, and not infrequently house sparrows, gather around to watch but never seem to butt in
during these disputes. At my feeding station in Virginia, starlings came in
large numbers only during and after snowfalls. At such times they swarmed

*Starlings maintaining individual distance*

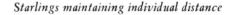

over feeders, fighting among themselves and keeping other birds away. For some reason, the starlings particularly resented the presence of most woodpeckers. A red-bellied woodpecker and sapsucker, on different occasions, were both turned over on their backs and savagely pecked. Flickers were accosted in much the same way, but other visitors, including downy woodpeckers, were largely ignored.

Like many other birds, starlings insist upon an "individual distance"—this is, the distance that each bird must be separated from its closest comrade if peaceful relations are to exist. Starlings illustrate this principle very nicely when they line up on overhead wires. Each bird will be at least three inches away from its nearest neighbor. Like ourselves, starlings do not care to be crowded too closely. When they are, they begin to fight.

Birdbanders must learn not to put starlings in the same holding cage with other birds. A birdbander on Cape Cod discovered to his dismay that half the dozen small birds he was holding were dead after being placed in the same cage with a starling. Piecing together what had happened, he concluded that the starling had pinned down one bird at a time and killed each with the usual blow at the back of the head. The victims were goldfinches and pine siskins.

In keeping with their stealthy natures, brown-headed cowbirds avoid fighting when it is on equal terms. While banding birds at Moose Hill, I never knew when a cowbird might attack a bird in a trap or even one I was holding. Once when I was holding two cowbirds too close to each other, one reached over with its bill and seized the other bird at a delicate spot just below the eye. A young hand-reared robin, getting its first taste of freedom on the lawn, was suddenly pounced upon by a cowbird that doubtless recognized an easy victim when it saw one. Luckily the robin shook itself free and flew off.

An even more one-sided case of aggression took place a few days later. I had released a cowbird in a neighboring town in a homing experiment. This bird, wearing a colored leg band, made it back safely, but, from the evidence I was able to piece together, straight into the jaws of a cat. Escaping with a broken wing, it attracted the attention of another cowbird. This bird, in the callous way that birds sometimes act when coming upon a stricken comrade, had the luckless individual on its back and was pounding its head when I hap-

pened upon the scene. I rescued the injured bird only to have it soon die of
its wounds.

I could give many more examples of sudden and often seemingly unpro-
voked aggression. We expect behavior of this kind in the cowbird, which lays
its eggs in other birds' nests and accepts none of the responsibilities of parent-
hood, and also in the house sparrow and starling. But what about the song
sparrow, which thrills us with its song and always acts the part of a good
parent? I'm afraid that even this highly regarded bird has its spells of excessive
belligerence. Every now and then one will try to dominate my feeding station
and for a while will succeed. William Brewster, in *October Farm,* tells how
one suddenly, for no obvious reason, launched a fierce attack upon a robin
engaged in searching for worms on the lawn. Rushing out in a kind of frenzy,
the song sparrow seized some of the robin's throat feathers in its bill and began
"hanging on like a bulldog." When last seen the robin was retreating and still
trying to shake off its adversary.

### Cannibalism

To descend to new depths in avian morality (if we can use this term with
birds), I'm afraid that I must point out that some birds, other than those
considered to be predators, are known to resort to cannibalism. Usually birds
are forced to this extreme only when a blizzard or some other disaster interferes
with their normal food supply. But turkey vultures in Jamaica, according to
Philip Henry Gosse,* in an account going back to the middle of the last century, are known to feast upon freshly shot comrades. This observation is
contrary to what most opinion holds, then and now. It is usually believed that
the turkey vulture will eat anything that is dead, no matter how repulsive it is,
except another of its kind. In a way it is too bad to shatter this one slightly
creditable feature in the vulture's revolting diet.

In an early issue of *The Auk,* Arthur T. Wayne tells of birds eating dead
birds in the wake of a blizzard in South Carolina in February 1899. Boat-
tailed grackles and red-winged blackbirds were eating dead fox sparrows and

* Philip Gosse, *Birds of Jamaica* (London: 1847).

killing and eating other fox sparrows that were numbed by the cold. Stronger living fox sparrows were eating their dead comrades.

A more recent example of cannibalism, involving boat-tailed grackles, occurred on the Carolina coast a few years ago and was not triggered by hard weather. Boat-tailed grackles took to dropping down on a bird feeder from an overhanging limb and attacking the yellow-rumped warblers that were feeding there. Before the horrified feeding-station operator had taken in what was happening, about a hundred of the warblers had been killed and their brains eaten.

During two late-spring snowstorms in Maine, there was large-scale cannibalism at bird feeders, according to Jerry Elwell in the July 1974 *Purple Martin News.* The crisis that forced some birds to cannibalism seemed partly related to a shortage of sunflower seeds. Pine siskins and other birds were competing at feeders with evening grosbeaks for the few that were left. In the melees that ensued, grosbeaks were seen to kill siskins and occasionally eat them. Cowbirds, as always revealing their worst sides, at times killed and devoured juncos. Elwell said that some of those maintaining bird feeders were so upset by what was happening that they couldn't sleep at night. One little lady was said to have moved her feeders to the edge of the woods so that she couldn't see what was taking place! Other species seen eating birds during this period were blue jays, starlings, red-wings, grackles, and meadowlarks.

That the first four should be involved should occasion no surprise in view of what has already been said about them. But the meadowlark hardly seems true to character when it dines on other birds. We think of it as an open-field bird with no questionable traits. But it is as much of a cannibal as the others when forced to extremes of hunger. A note by John and Claudia Hubbard in a 1969 issue of *Bird-Banding* tells of meadowlarks feeding on road-killed birds along a highway in New Mexico during near-blizzard conditions. In one instance, a meadowlark was feeding on another meadowlark. According to Mrs. C. F. Austin, in a letter to *Purple Martin News,* a meadowlark during severe cold and snow in Kentucky was seen eating another bird and trying to capture first a towhee and then a cardinal.

Adding another species to this rather dismal tally, John C. Watkins in a

1960 issue of *The Chat* reported a covey of quail feeding on a dead robin during a hard winter in South Carolina.

The grackle's unsavory habit of killing house sparrows, and sometimes other birds, and eating their brains has been known since early in this century. Horace Wright, in his booklet "Birds of the Boston Public Gardens," noted grackle predation upon house sparrows back in 1909. He suspected that the grackles were retaliating because of the thieving propensities of the house sparrow. Even the food that the grackles were taking to their young was sometimes stolen by the house sparrows. Nearly every year, I find a dead house sparrow or two in my yard with the head severed, the brains and part of the body eaten. These are usually young birds recently out of the nest. Squeamish feeding-station operators would prefer not to have these executions and their gruesome aftermath taking place on their lawns. The house sparrows, on their part, never seem to learn. They continue to feed confidently alongside the grackles and snatch their food whenever the opportunity offers.

In England, house sparrows have an unexpected enemy in the form of the mallard duck. According to Neil Ardley in his book *Birds of Towns,** mallards, beginning in 1929, began catching house sparrows for food. After seizing a house sparrow in its bill, the mallard would take its struggling victim to the nearest body of water, hold it under until it had drowned, and then, after expertly plucking the feathers, would eat it. The novel method of execution by drowning is sometimes utilized by other bird species. In the November 1979 issue of *American Birds,* for example, there are accounts of both a Cooper's hawk and a marsh hawk drowning their respective victims.

During hard weather the common grackle, whose low tastes have already been mentioned, may considerably expand its brand of cannibalism by eating dead birds of other species as well as its own dead. I had heard of this occurring when many birds are killed along highways during winter snowstorms. I saw my first large-scale grackle cannibalism during the heavy snows of 1979, when thousands of birds left the fields near where I was living in Maryland to forage for spilled grain along cleared roadsides. As the snow and cold continued and

---

* Neil Ardley, *Birds of Towns* (New Malden, Surrey, England: Almark Publishing, 1975).

food became ever scarcer, the famished birds were killed by the hundreds by road traffic. Several hundred, mostly grackles and red-wings, were killed along a few miles of highway near my abode. Grackles began eating dead grackles and other dead birds. I saw literally dozens of instances of this. Cannibalism was also observed on a smaller scale among the red-wings, and I saw four starlings eating a dead pigeon.

Putting aside moralistic sentiment, which should be reserved only for us humans, I could hardly blame the birds during this dire time for eating their fellows. They had no other choice unless it was starvation. As soon as the snow had melted enough for birds to resume their normal feeding, they went back to the open fields and the cannibalism ceased entirely. I drew from this the conclusion that birds do not relish eating their own kind or close relatives.

*House sparrow snatching a worm from a robin*

## Theft

Since thievery is a pursuit that takes a certain amount of skill and daring, it is not birds that are most in need that steal but those that are most competent. Frequently thievery is a game that serves as relief from more routine activities. If a chickadee detects some other bird taking food from the bird feeder and storing it in a nearby hiding place, it will almost invariably go to this food instead of the easily procured food at the feeder. To give another example of pilfering stores, besides those in the earlier chapter on food, a black-capped chickadee at Moose Hill used to follow a white-breasted nuthatch to its caches, remove the food, and drop it to the ground. Becoming more responsible, this bird began storing food on its own.

Not many birds will attempt to steal the food some other bird is eating. To do so would invite retaliation. Yet the house sparrow brazenly tries to take food from birds much larger than it is. Among its intended victims are the already mentioned grackles and starlings. These birds not infrequently return the compliment by stealing food from house sparrows. The grackle, of course, sometimes goes a step further, killing the thief and eating choice parts. The grim warning seems to have no effect upon the house sparrows. They stubbornly go right on stealing the grackle's food whenever they can.

Olive Thorne Miller, in her book, *A Bird Lover in the West,*[*] tells how house sparrows snatch corn from the beaks of cardinals and grackles. We see house sparrows doing this at our feeders today. The cardinal, along with starlings, grackles, and occasionally red-wings, is singled out for this treatment. Out on the lawn, house sparrows indulge in another kind of food snatching. Individual house sparrows or several at a time closely watch robins, waiting for one to begin pulling a worm. As soon as the worm is out of the ground, a house sparrow will rush in and seize it. The baffled robin quickly goes back to worm hunting again. There is a record of house sparrows seizing no less than six worms in succession from the same robin.

As if to prove that they will stop at nothing in the way of underhanded tricks, house sparrows have been known to snatch food out of the mouths of

---

* Olive Thorne Miller, *A Bird Lover in the West* (Boston and New York: Houghton, Mifflin & Co., 1900).

baby birds. J. K. Jensen tells of such an incident in a 1925 issue of *The Auk*. When a parent robin in a yard in New Mexico was carrying food to its brood, a pair of house sparrows would follow it all the way to the nest and wait for the feeding operation to begin. At the precise moment that food was placed in the gaping mouth of a youngster, one of the sparrows would seize it and fly away. This was literally snatching food out of the mouths of babes!

Somewhat less imaginative than house sparrows but on to many of the same tricks, other birds sometimes make a practice of food snatching. A bird-bander in Ohio noticed that house sparrows were clever enough to enter one of his banding traps, seize a piece of bread, and then find their way out without being caught. Their enterprise went for nothing when grackles were in attendance. Waiting on the outside for the house sparrow to make its exit would be a grackle ready to harass the bird and make it drop its bread. There are also records of grackles, as well as starlings, watching robins on the lawn and taking worms from them in the same way as house sparrows. A brown thrasher was also seen doing this.

Somewhat less subtle are the tactics of birds at feeding stations when a larger, more proficient seed-opener is eating sunflower seeds. The small bird rushes in at the right moment and either takes the opened seed out of the beak of its victim or picks up small pieces as they fall. Goldfinches and pine siskins prey upon purple finches in this way, and, I suspect, sometimes dare play this trick on the more imposing evening grosbeak. A northern oriole, wintering on Cape Cod, learned how to take seeds from the beaks of purple finches. And white-throated sparrows, scratching among sunflower hulls on the ground below my Droll Yankee feeder, discovered that it was easier to steal sound seeds from the beaks of house finches than find their own. They stopped short of attempting this on evening grosbeaks, however.

After this recitation about theft in the bird world, it may come as a surprise to learn of birds' returning food that they did not eat. But first let me say that we should hesitate to make moral judgements when birds are guilty of acts that we frown upon. Their behavior is not determined by ethics but the rules of survival. A blue jay surprised me one day by returning uneaten food to my bird feeder. Whether from higher motives or not (probably not), the jay returned a piece of cake that it had carried away seconds earlier. After dropping it at approximately the place where it had been, the bird flew away without further ado.

### The infirm

The kindly treatment mentioned in the previous chapter, in which an evening grosbeak befriended an ailing member of its flock and blue jays cared for an aged individual, are exceptions to the rule. Normally the best an ailing bird can look forward to is total indifference. No longer an accepted member of the flock, it gets along as best it can. These outcasts frequently turn up at feeding stations. They haunt the nearest shrubbery and come out to feed when competition is less keen. If the bird recovers, chances are that it will again be accepted by its comrades. This was the case with a male Carolina chickadee that, according to Martin A. Slessers in a 1970 *Atlantic Naturalist*, was ostracized by other chickadees when it had a raw wound from the loss of an eye. Not only this, the bird was so frequently harassed by other chickadees and tufted titmice that it had to forsake the feeders and forage for itself in nearby woodland. But in time the wound healed and the bird was accepted back into the flock. Although awkward in its movements, the partially blind bird obtained a mate and helped rear a family.

Ailing birds that I have played host to at my Maryland bird feeder have included evening grosbeaks, cowbirds, and grackles. These pensioners spent their entire time in the immediate vicinity of the feeder. Scuttling away at any sign of danger, the birds—sometimes three or four of them—led reasonably sheltered existences. A lame cowbird was sometimes chased by blue jays and on one occasion was pursued by a pigeon. Another lame cowbird, so far as I could tell, was ignored by other birds.

It would be easy to get the impression that the same ailing birds spend the entire winter at a feeding station. In some instances, this may be true. Several of the same superannuated grackles seemed to appear at my Maryland feeders every winter. But many times the ailing bird is killed by a cat, dog, or small-bird hawk and therefore has a tenure at the feeder of only a few weeks at the most. As individuals die or are killed, other incapacitated birds wander in to take their place. In winter there always seems to be a floating population of these forlorn outcasts. Thus the number seen at bird feeders may stay relatively stable. By late spring, survivors will usually have departed. The occasional bird that can make it on its own may wander back the following fall.

Although almost any infirm or oddly colored bird, including albinos and partial albinos, are shunned by others in the flock and sometimes set upon, the crippled or famished hawk that visits a feeding station is scarcely noticed. This was true of a red-tailed hawk at a feeder in Virginia and another in Kentucky; also, according to Roy Ivor, small birds ignored a red-tail at a feeder in Canada. Cardinals and house sparrows fed almost at the feet of a wounded black vulture recuperating in a yard in Florida. On the other hand, a red-tailed hawk with badly swollen feet at a bird feeder in Massachusetts was heckled by grackles.

### Thwarting troublemakers

Birds, as we have seen in the previous chapter, take precautions to escape their enemies. But they can't spend most of their lives flying away from danger or hiding. Their lives are busy enough with finding food and other activities. The hustle and bustle of the feeding station, with its sometimes overbearing or aggressive members, can't deter birds either. They must find ways to eat without constantly being set upon. Thanks to a variety of ruses, nearly every bird does receive its share, but not without a certain amount of inconvenience.

Flying off after being rebuffed at the feeder is one way birds avoid a troublemaker. As long as the bird can fly a short distance and perhaps come back to a less crowded or less well-protected part of the feeder, little time or energy has been lost. Birds constantly resort to this simple ruse. However, there is one catch in this. Flying off seems frequently to arouse an instinct in the aggressor to pursue. The robin that for a while dominated my bird feeder in Florida used to chase other birds for long distances. Yellow-rumped warblers and song sparrows always seem to give chase when in an aggressive mood. In early August, a male cardinal at my Virginia feeding station began pursuing other birds that came for food.

Pursuing other birds is also a common practice in the wild. Mention has already been made of mobbing enemies. In a less serious way, one or more small birds will sally forth in pursuit of a much larger bird in what looks more like sport or exercise of skills than anything else. City dwellers not infrequently see a house sparrow flying directly behind a pigeon as if trying to overtake the larger bird. Who hasn't seen a red-winged blackbird, a hummingbird, or an eastern kingbird in pursuit of a crow or hawk?

The playful attack of the eastern kingbird can turn into serious business when the quarry is overtaken. In a display of skill and daring, a kingbird may sometimes alight on the back of a flying crow or hawk and begin delivering sharp blows at the larger bird's head. This is little more than an annoyance to the larger bird, which normally quickly shakes off its pursuer. But according to William Brewster, a robin was overtaken over a river by an eastern kingbird and received a dozen or more blows on the back of the head. So terrified was the robin that it began squealing, in the words of Brewster, as though in the clutches of a hawk. Brewster also speaks of two occasions when he saw an eastern kingbird overtake a chimney swift.

Not all kingbird attacks are so spectacular. I saw a kingbird repeatedly sally forth after individuals in a flock of goldfinches that was feeding nearby. No harm was done, so I assumed that this was play or a test of skills on the part of the kingbird.

"Getting lost in the crowd" when rebuffed at the bird feeder is another way birds get away from a domineering bird. When large numbers of birds are feeding together, most squabbles quickly come to an end when one of the contestants backs away and loses itself among the other birds. Lower-ranking purple finches are particularly apt to resort to this measure. Painted buntings at a feeding station maintained some years ago by Clara Bates in Fort Pierce, Florida, had this stratagem down to a fine art. Whenever any members of the flock were challenged by a mourning dove, they quickly slipped behind the dove, where they couldn't be seen, and went on feeding.

In spite of their occasional bloody conflicts, painted buntings can show intelligence in accommodating themselves to difficult situations. At a feeding station in South Carolina, I observed how one male bunting waited in a bush while its rival, another male, fed. Never did the two feed together. They avoided conflicts by staying away from each other. Their approach was similar to the one used by a hairy woodpecker at my bird feeder in Virginia. When starlings were present, this woodpecker used to hide behind one of the posts supporting the feeder and wait there until its foes had departed.

By visiting bird feeders very early, a number of birds find peaceful conditions and avoid enemies. Early-morning feeding is an established routine among pheasants, ruffed grouse, cardinals, evening grosbeaks, juncos, and white-throated sparrows. Evening grosbeaks have been recorded at feeders so early that it was difficult to distinguish them in the dim light. Many of these same species, particularly cardinals and white-throats, also have late feeding hours. Feeding-station operators should encourage these early and late visitors by having sufficient food available for them. Spreading out the feeding hours helps make for less crowding and better chances for all to share in the feast.

Another way that birds avoid competition at feeders is by eating higher or lower. These tactics worked perfectly at a South Carolina feeder heavily patronized by red-winged blackbirds and cowbirds. The red-wings fed at a raised feeder, while on the ground cowbirds fed upon grain scattered by the red-wings. The two species never mingled or attempted to feed at the other's "preserve." Yet in the wild and also at other feeders, cowbirds, red-wings, and other members of the blackbird family do feed together. Perhaps an uneasy truce exists when this occurs and the birds would really prefer segregated feeding. At a feeder in Florida, red-wings fed on the ground while grackles fed at a raised feeder.

If competition becomes too severe at bird feeders, some members of the feeding flock may leave for good. This is an unlikely alternative for permanent residents or birds that characteristically stay all winter or all summer. These residents stay and suffer unless there is a less crowded bird feeder in a neighboring yard that they can go to. On the other hand, birds that normally wander anyway during the nonbreeding season simply move on if conditions do not suit them. We are usually only too glad to see roving flocks of starlings, grackles, cowbirds, or red-wings leave us for good. The finches are more popular. We may be reluctant to see them go. When grackles and cowbirds arrived at my Maryland feeders during a spell of wintry weather, the evening grosbeaks departed. I would have preferred to have had it the other way around. When playing host to both goldfinches and pine siskins, I've had one species or the other abruptly leave. The two compete too heavily for the same foods and the same places at bird feeders.

Two other species that do not mix comfortably together are house finches and purple finches. Again, it seems to be a matter of eating the same foods and at the same places. Since the great population boom of the house finch in the East (all are birds descended from a few released in the New York City area in 1941), there have been complaints that purple finches are not seen as often at bird feeders. Perhaps they avoid feeders that are overly well patronized by house finches. Although house finches are mild-mannered birds, they do have a way of taking up space and monopolizing the food supply.

This is the same complaint exactly that has been leveled against the house sparrow when it appears at bird feeders. A bully when it comes to usurping the nesting sites of other birds, the house sparrow is on the other hand not overly aggressive when eating. Even back in 1914, during its heyday, the house sparrow was described in an issue of *Bird-Lore* as feeding peacefully with other birds at bird feeders. One song sparrow could chase off three house sparrows. Its behavior is much the same today. Margaret Millar, in her book *The Birds and Beasts Were There*,* describes the house sparrow as not having a special relationship with any of its fellow boarders. It starts eating, she writes, without any preliminaries, "polite or impolite," and ignores other birds.

The difficulty with house sparrows at bird feeders is that so often there are too many of them. They eat almost everything and take the space and vantage points that we would rather see go to more desirable species. But now that the house finch is coming ever more into ascendancy, house sparrows, like purple finches, are staying away from feeders. At least this is my impression based upon observations at a number of feeding stations. Also in many areas, particularly in the East, the house sparrow has declined in numbers to a point where it is very much in the minority. Disease in the form of salmonella has thinned the house sparrow's ranks, while nearly everything you can think of preys upon this species, which must rank as a great delicacy in the animal world.

As a result, the house sparrow today is far from being the rampant, all-

---

* Margaret Millar, *The Birds and Beasts Were There* (New York: Random House, 1967).

conquering species that it once was. Many find advantages in having this bird. Whether a willing host or not, the house sparrow is often joined by other birds that are new to an area. A western tanager at Bucksport, Maine, stood off starlings but fed with house sparrows. The dickcissels that turn up along the Atlantic coast in fall and winter and that so often find feeding stations almost invariably become associated with house sparrows. An escaped cage bird is more likely to join house sparrows than birds of any other species. An escaped budgerigar will come to a feeder with house sparrows, leave abruptly when they do, and visit the birdbath and go to roost at night with its new comrades. Such an attachment is a means of survival for any bird that suddenly finds itself in a strange climate, with no knowledge of enemies, food, or where to spend the night. The house sparrow had to find out these facts for itself during its early days on this continent.

# Habitat and Food Plants | 7

When banding birds at the farm in Virginia, I became interested in finding out which of several likely habitats would produce the largest catch. Bird-banders are motivated as much by numbers as anything else. If you catch and band large numbers of birds, it stands to reason that you will obtain more data in the way of longevity records, birds returning another year, and recoveries beyond the immediate banding area. There is also an element of competition. You look forward to being able to tell another birdbander that you are ahead of your last year's banding totals. The motivation is much the same as that which drives the bird lister to exceed his previous scores.

In the interest of catching more birds, I decided to trap simultaneously in four different habitats and compare the results. An overgrown fencerow proved to be slightly more productive than a weed patch. This was not unexpected. No matter what time of the year it is, the fencerow with its luxuriant growth is always teeming with birds. During a period from late November until mid-January, birds most commonly taken in fencerow habitat were tufted titmice, cardinals, dark-eyed juncos, and tree sparrows.

The reason the fencerow is overgrown is that the birds themselves did the planting. After eating fruits of such plants as flowering dogwood, sassafras, red cedar, wild cherry, blackberry, and Japanese honeysuckle, birds very often repair to a fenceline to sit and digest their food. Some of the hard seeds and pits are coughed up, while others pass through the digestive system and are voided. Soon the ground below is dotted with young plants that owe their presence to birds. In time birds benefit from the shelter, nesting sites, and food that the new growth affords. As the plants mature, birds begin transporting the seeds to still other locations. Eventually, unless the process is checked, the countryside begins to revert into a young forest, in early stages made up of bird-transported plants. With the decline in farming that has taken place throughout much of the East during the last one hundred years, vast areas once open are now timbered. Birds for the most part have benefited, although I could list a number of open-country birds, like the vesper sparrow, that are losing out.

The next best habitat on our farm for catching birds was a weed patch in an overgrown vegetable garden. Unlike the fencerow, this was a temporary habitat that drew birds only during the fall and winter. A good crop of lamb's-quarters was responsible for the presence of large flocks of juncos and tree sparrows. The dead stalks offered cover, while the mature seed heads offered food. Birds frequenting this habitat came readily to traps baited with sunflower and scratch feed.

Only a stone's throw away, across the lane to the house, was rich hardwood forest stretching from river bluffs to upland fields. Among oaks, hickory, red

*Hummingbirds are attracted to the showy blossoms of trumpet creeper.*

cedar, and honeysuckle, I established my third trapping area. Here I caught only about half as many birds as I did in either of the other two habitats. Woodland is never as rewarding to the birdbander and bird-watcher as more open country. Nevertheless, many birds do congregate at the edge where trees meet open fields. In woodland close to this borderline habitat, my catch consisted mostly of tufted titmice, juncos, and tree sparrows; also a few red-bellied woodpeckers.

I recognized that my fourth habitat held little promise. This was a nearby pasture where the only cover was tufts of grass no more than a few inches high. Since this was an experiment, I placed my traps here anyway. My only captures were one cardinal and five equally bold juncos, which, overcoming their fear of anything as conspicuous as a wire-mesh banding trap, had entered anyway. The same boldness would be required of birds coming to feeding stations far from cover. This is why I insist upon having adequate escape cover near my bird feeders.

So far as I can, I try to duplicate fencerow conditions in parts of my garden. My lawn is the equivalent of pasture or cultivated field, while the ornamental plantings around the house and along borders with neighbors are the equivalent of overgrown fencerows. The combination works very well. I have birds and other wildlife, privacy, and natural beauty. But I must guard against overplanting. It is edge effect that is most attractive to birdlife—trees giving way to shrubs, still lower growth, and finally lawn. At least some of the yard should be in lawns, walkways, driveway, flower and vegetable plots.

### Fencerow plants

I can't remember when the idea first occurred to me, but years ago I began bringing fencerow plants into the yard on the theory that if they were what attracted birds in the wild, I might as well make use of them. Friends, who visualized the fencerow as an overgrown tangle of poison ivy, Japanese honeysuckle, and briers, were aghast at my bad taste. They didn't realize that the fencerow harbors a number of plants that are choice stock at nurseries. I have already mentioned the presence of red cedar and flowering dogwood in fencerows, and there are others that show up to good advantage in any yard.

Fencerow plants will be more drought- and disease-resistant than most plants we could buy. They will be adapted to our local soil and climate conditions, and there can scarcely be a doubt about their value to birds. The question is, which of these plants are best suited for the more demanding conditions of the home? Not only bird appeal enters into our choice, but, needless to say, a plant can't be too weedlike or too much of an ugly duckling if it is to adorn our yard.

I like the sumacs for their picturesque habit and brilliant fall coloring. But they do have a propensity for growing ever outward from the original cluster. Under proper management, sumacs are ideal for accenting the lines of a modern ranch-style home, and I've seen them used effectively in small city yards. Even more rampant are the woody vines that are so much a part of fencerow vegetation. We should avoid poison ivy, of course, in spite of the popularity of the berries with winter birds, and substitute instead another good bird plant, Virginia Creeper, that is much better behaved and has no toxic effects. Trained against a wall or side of a house, this woody fencerow vine will eventually blanket a surface in much the same way as English ivy. The brilliant red leaves in the fall and dark-blue berries make such a magnificent display that one wonders why the vine isn't planted more often. I have nothing against English ivy except for the way it has of running riot over everything. Birds start eating the berries of this ivy in the fall and continue to do so through the winter as long as the supply lasts.

I would hesitate to recommend wild grape, another sprawling fencerow vine, for the same reason I have reservations about English ivy. It is of interest, however, that many of our cultivated grapes were derived from our wild muscadine and fox grapes. Birds like grapes only too well and sometimes can be seen picking at dried ones still clinging to stems in early winter. Still another fencerow vine to consider is trumpet creeper. Shabby-looking in winter and likely to get out of hand, the creeper has one enormous advantage—its gorgeous orange to red trumpet-shaped flowers are the delight of hummingbirds and gardeners alike. Would that the plant were a little less aggressive!

The real enchantment of flowering dogwood happens in spring when the immaculate white blooms brighten the still-wintry landscape. On our farm we had the added spectacle of redbud coming into bloom at the same time as dogwood. Neither plant has much to offer birds in the way of cover or nesting sites. But in the fall, flowering dogwoods offer a second display—clusters of bright-red berries that last only too short a time if discovered by flocks of birds. When cedar waxwings or grackles were in the trees eating the berries, we would hear a patter as though of falling hail. The noise was from discarded pits or stones hitting leaf litter on the ground below. The red berries wouldn't have lasted anyway. They darken and fall off with the arrival of cold weather.

I must admit that the nurseries offer better hollies than anything we can find in the fencrow. The scraggly American holly rescued from entwining poison ivy or Japanese honeysuckle is unlikely to add to the beauty of the yard. Unless it is a female plant that will produce berries, it isn't going to add to the bird's food supply either. Hollies of all kinds are excellent for birds and ornament, but we might as well get the best if we are going to have them in our yards. I feel the same way about sassafras and persimmon. In the fencerow they are pleasing to the eye; in the yard they are ungainly and unsure of themselves. After thorough ripening under the influence of cold weather, persimmon fruit loses its astringency. As a boy, I only too often experienced the

*The red berries of the flowering dogwood are an autumn food source for birds.*

puckering effect of unripe fruit. Both sassafras and persimmon are popular with birds. A friend in Kentucky reported no less than forty bird species feeding on sassafras fruits in her yard during one season.

I hesitate to recommend multiflora rose in the yard because of its overly luxuriant growth and the way birds, dropping the seeds, establish new plants wherever there is uncared-for ground. Farmers, although they use the plant as a living fence that will hold livestock and for food and cover for wildlife, have the same objection to the plant. We planted multiflora along fencerows on our farm, and I always have a few plants in my yard. Unlike cultivated roses, this one takes no care and birds are still eating the small red hips in late winter.

The tree that comes closest to having the same wildlife values as multiflora is red cedar. It is the plant *par excellence* for nesting sites and dense cover. The small blue berries, if not devoured by birds, sometimes stay on the trees all year. If the fencerow red cedar is a little too scrubby, there are more than enough horticultural varieties, often called junipers, to fit every landscaping need.

Finally, elderberry and pokeweed shouldn't be banished simply because they are too weedlike. I find enough beauty in both plants to permit them in my yard. Elderberry, with its clusters of juicy berries, is popular with both birds and wine and jelly makers. Pokeweed is suspected of being slightly poisonous, but the black, juicy berries are so well liked by birds that I refrain from removing the occasional plant that springs up in my yard. Another asset of poke, as it

*One of the best trees to attract birds, the red cedar provides food, shelter, and nesting sites.*

is sometimes called, are the tender shoots in spring, which are perfectly safe for human consumption when boiled and taste like asparagus.

### Late harvests

Every winter a few fruits and seeds come through unscathed enough to furnish food for birds during the food-scarce period of spring. Still clinging to plants, they have weathered winter storms and cold, and, to varying degrees, the appetites of birds. How can one account for such tenacity? Is this something the plant kingdom has devised over the ages to better distribute the seed crop?

While many seeds will find their way into the soil in the fall and sprout as soon as warm weather returns, the plant may find advantages in holding its seeds for longer periods of time. If seeds are retained through the winter, there are not so many losses in the ground from weather and the appetites of animals. Many pines and other cone-bearing trees and shrubs have solved this problem by keeping seeds safely in cones through part of the winter or longer. Longleaf pine holds its seeds until late fall and early winter. Pitch pine begins shedding its seeds in midwinter, while Scotch pine waits until early May. Among the spruces, larches, birches, and alders can be found other examples of late shedding. The alders (*Alnus*), whose seeds are so well favored by goldfinches, redpolls, and pine siskins, slowly lose their seeds over a period of five months from October until the end of March. If plants could be given awards for being of service to birds during the colder months of the year, I would favor one going to the alders.

Birds are on to hidden food supplies found in the cones of various evergreen and deciduous plants. As soon as outside scales begin to part enough for them to insert their bills, they begin feasting. The crossbills, as well as tree squirrels, do not have to wait. They begin prying or breaking into cones long before they have opened. While some birds dig seeds out of opening cones, others, like juncos, wait on the ground below for fallen seeds. If the winter cone harvest in the North is a good one, many of the nomadic finches stay where they are instead of moving southward.

Maples of several kinds also hold their harvest long enough to assist birds during the colder months. The paired winged seeds, known as keys, sometimes cling to the trees through the winter and into early spring. This is true of sycamore maple and box elder. Evening grosbeaks are so fond of the keys of box elder that during some years they seem to shape their migrations around the supply. This does not stop them from visiting feeding stations for their favorite sunflower. The pine grosbeak is the only other major consumer of maple keys among the birds. Several of the ashes, with their winged seeds or samaras, also furnish winter food for grosbeaks.

Some plants get around the necessity of holding their harvest all winter by early flowering, quickly followed by maturing and shedding of seeds. Most elms, including the well-known American elm, fall in this group. The early species begin to bloom in April or May. Soon small winged seeds appear that are the delight of goldfinches. River birch follows the example of the elms by blooming early and shedding seeds in late spring and early summer.

Fruit-bearing trees and shrubs, for the most part, have already offered their harvest to birds by the time winter gets underway. If some of the fruit manages to cling to twigs all winter, this is more an accident than a design of nature. Nevertheless in the North there are usually enough late fruits and berries to sustain robins, waxwings, yellow-rumped warblers, and even bluebirds through the winter. Near the coast, if the crop is good, bayberry furnishes a good harvest for overwintering birds. As far north as Nova Scotia and south

*The pitch pine begins shedding its seeds in midwinter.*

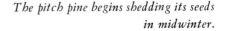

to Georgia, winterberry (*Ilex verticillata*) helps maintain robins and other birds through the winter. Highbush cranberry, bittersweet (*Celastrus scandens*), and leftover apples, rotten though they be, are other fruits that help sustain winter birdlife in more northern regions. In the latitude of Maryland and Virginia, Japanese honeysuckle, multiflora rose, sumac, Virginia creeper, poison ivy, hackberry, red cedar, and various of the privets and hollies are among the most important mainstays of fruit-eating birds in winter. Southward from the Carolinas to Florida and Texas, a number of other plants, including yaupon holly, mistletoe, pyracantha, and nandina, can be added to the list.

Why is it that plants like these hold their harvests over part of the winter, while others, like flowering dogwood, mountain ash, and most viburnums, rarely have anything left to show by Christmas? Abundant fruiting, coupled with ability of fruits to withstand cold and remain attached to branches, would seem to provide a large share of the answer. If the plant is a heavy producer, it will take birds longer to harvest the crop. Add to this such factors as pithiness, astringency, and hardness and we find still other reasons why some of the crop is left until later. Even if birds bolt down most fruits without tasting them, there are subtle influences that affect their choice. Although it may be hard for us to put our finger on exactly what it is, we do know that some seeds and grain disappear much faster than others at the feeding station. In the same way, some fruits disappear almost at once, while others hang on all winter. Sometimes birds will strip one berry-bearing tree of its fruit and leave a neighboring tree of the same species untouched. Vagaries such as these make actions of birds in the wild as interesting as those we see at feeding stations. Luckily, enough fruits, and, as we have already seen, maple keys, pine seeds, and the like remain well into winter, a time of the year when food of this kind is most needed.

Japanese honeysuckle, for example, is only mildly tempting to birds in the fall but comes under increasingly heavy attack as other foods diminish in January and February. Usually in my part of Maryland, white-throated sparrows are finishing the last of the honeysuckle berries by the end of February and are beginning to turn more to weed seeds and sumac.

I have observed the same sequence of events in multiflora rose, except that the bright-red hips are taken by birds earlier and some always remain on the plant until well into spring. Multiflora is such a prolific producer that birds cannot possibly eat their way through the harvest in a short period of time. But this isn't the only explanation why multiflora is so long-lasting. The hips, or many of them, are not easy for birds to reach. The slender branchlets are likely to give way under the weight of a bird the size of a robin or starling. Unless the bird quickly springs into flight, it may find itself entangled in the thorny interior of the bush. I have seen cautious robins reach out from a safe perch in a plant of another kind to obtain a share of the harvest.

Multiflora, being a choice winter food of mockingbirds, sometimes comes under the guardianship of this bird. A possessive mockingbird will bitterly fight off all other birds in its attempts to safeguard its winter food supply. Although it is not always successful in keeping bushes to itself, a determined mockingbird is still another reason why rose hips are still present on bushes by spring. Mockingbirds are equally determined in protecting a wide variety of other fruit-bearing plants.

Hackberries seem to survive the early onslaughts of birds for some of the same reasons that multiflora does. To reach berries near tips of slender twigs, birds frequently have to flutter on rapidly beating wings. Cedar waxwings can do this gracefully enough, but it is a difficult feat for robins and many other of the birds that feast on the black, sweet-tasting berries. One winter in Kansas a large crop was still on the trees in mid-March. The food attracted hundreds of robins and cedar waxwings which were nearly famished because virtually all other natural foods had been exhausted by this late date.

Sumacs are sometimes regarded as emergency foods that birds wouldn't eat unless desperately hungry. I find that this is far from being the case. Even when other foods are abundant, I have observed widespread use by birds of sumac. Although the fruit consists largely of a single seed, birds seem undaunted by this. Louise Mullen, a Vermont bird observer, tells me that where she lives, birds come to the plants more for bugs that infest the seeds than anything the fruit has to offer. She says that by March evening grosbeaks and over-wintering robins have generally cleaned out the supply. Seed clusters of sumac can be used successfully in supplementing the food supply at feeding stations.

Greenbrier (*Smilax*) is like sumac in being mostly seed and skin. If plants are too stingy in offering rewards, birds won't eat the fruits and thus the plant loses essential help in establishing itself elsewhere. Apparently greenbrier offers just enough to birds to obtain this essential help. It is difficult to walk about in many woodland areas in the East because of the dense tangles of greenbrier. That the plant isn't overly popular with birds is seen in the many berries that remain on the spiny stems after the winter and spring harvest season is over.

Privets are somewhat more liberal in their rewards. Where I live in Maryland, it is always a race to see whether privet or Japanese honeysuckle is stripped first by birds. Japanese honeysuckle usually wins. For those who grow privet, the bushes should not be clipped so severely that plants will be left without blossoms and fruit. Border privet (*Ligustrum obtusifolium*) and its variety Regel privet are good privets for late-winter bird use. Apparently birds find other fruits more to their liking in the fall, and therefore privet, with its usual heavy crop of berries, is available during the food-scarce time that comes later.

People, as well as birds, it can be assumed, are more aware of the hollies in winter than almost any other plants. The eye-catching red of American holly, winterberry, and yaupon holly is enough to draw attention to these three popular native species. The exotic English and Chinese hollies, also with red berries, are equally in demand for landscaping. Not quite as conspicuous are hollies with black berries. Our inkberry (*Ilex glabra*) is a handsome black-fruited species, and so is Japanese holly. The latter keeps its fruits well into

*Pine siskin taking seeds from the cones of alder*

winter, a time of the year when they are most needed by birds. Sexes are on separate plants in hollies so that it is essential for fruiting to have both staminate and pistillate plants in the near vicinity of each other.

Why birds so often pass up the hollies in the fall and only slowly begin to eat the fruit in winter and spring is still another of the tantalizing questions that surround the harvesting of fruit and berry crops by birds. Eric Simms, in his book *British Thrushes*,* states that the English holly (*Ilex aquifolium*) has two seasons of usage by thrushes. One is in the autumn and the other in May and June. This would seem to suggest that the berries aren't overly tart or astringent; otherwise birds probably wouldn't be eating them in the fall. I have tasted, and promptly spat out, berries of our American holly in early and late fall. I didn't experience any very unpleasant taste, and birds, much less sensitive in regard to taste than I am, shouldn't be bothered either. Yet the fruit of American holly is not normally taken by birds until December and, as a rule, plants are still heavily decked with berries in April and May. Chinese holly, with even larger, more showy berries, is ordinarily the very last of the winter fruits taken by birds in the South. Winterberry is consumed much earlier. On Nantucket, robins and other birds begin flocking to bushes for the red berries in late October.

None of the explanations I have offered for delayed use of fruits by birds seems to apply to the hollies, except astringency. But as I reported in the chapter on food, wild birds do not seem to be deterred, or only slightly, from taking foods because of bitterness or astringency. Even in summer, when fruits and berries are in good supply, birds eagerly take the astringent fruits of a number of plants, including chokecherry.

Something about the red-fruited hollies, however, seems to keep birds from downing the fruits until quite late in fall or even until late winter or early spring. The same is true to varying degrees of a number of other shrubs with red or orange fruits. In this list I would include nandina, pyracantha, Japanese barberry, Amur honeysuckle, American and European highbush cranberry, and two or three of the cotoneasters. While several of these plants have pithy or

* Eric Simms, *British Thrushes* (London: Collins, 1978).

astringent fruits, there must be some other reason or reasons why birds are
sometimes slow about taking the fruit.

Whatever it is that slows them, we enjoy the bright display the fruits
provide and birds have the advantage of a source of food during the difficult
period of winter scarcity. Still another plus about these long-lasting fruits is
that starlings rarely ever eat them.

Finally, if I had space in my yard for only one more sizable plant, I would
choose one of the crab apples. Ozumi crab apple (*Malus zumi* var. *calocarpa*)
has small red fruits that ripen in late fall and that hang on into winter as long
as the birds will allow. Another excellent crab apple for birds in winter is the
"Bob White" variety of Siberian crab (*Malus baccata*). Its small yellow fruits
are well-liked by birds, an exception to the rule that birds generally prefer
red fruits to yellow ones. The crab apples, besides supplying birds with food and
us with jellies, have the added advantage of a spring floral display that compares
favorably with that of any of the flowering fruit trees.

*Winterberry holly provides birds with a
ready source of food through the
winter months.*

*Buds and blossoms*

Many birds do not wait for next year's crop. Beginning in early winter, they start feeding on the small buds that, if left intact, would eventually turn into flowers and finally, after pollination, into fruit. The bud eaters, including grouse, blue jays, waxwings, house sparrows, and many of the finches, apparently derive enough nourishment from buds to keep them suitably fed during times of scarcity. In England, it has been found that the bullfinch, the greatest bud eater of all, can survive well on buds from the end of February until the fruiting season. Prior to this time, the smaller, less developed buds do not provide enough nourishment to form the exclusive diet of the bullfinch. According to research conducted by Ian Newton, author of *Finches,** when ash trees produce good crops, which is every other year, bullfinches eat the winged seeds and far fewer buds. During alternate years, when there are few ash seeds to fall back on, flocks of bullfinches enter orchards and begin systematically stripping trees of their buds. Plums and pears suffer most, followed

* Ian Newton, *Finches* (London: Collins, 1972).

*Birds feed upon bittersweet until
late March.*

by gooseberries and currants, and finally apples and cherries. Fruit growers, as might be expected, sometimes suffer severe losses. While it may be little comfort to them, birds can take half the buds from a pear tree without decreasing the yield, and this follows to varying degrees with buds of other trees and shrubs.

We have no bud eater as destructive as the bullfinch on our side of the Atlantic, for which we can be grateful. Many of our birds do have the habit, however, and yearly do a good share of bud pruning on fruit trees and yard ornamentals. Whether or not this pruning is harmful depends upon how thorough the birds are. According to accounts in Bent's *Life Histories,* pruning of buds on apple trees by ruffed grouse resulted in trees producing better crops. The same was true of apple and pear trees pruned by purple finches. Bent succinctly sums up the pros and cons of the habit by saying, "It is an open question whether blossom eating and budding is harmful to the trees or beneficial as proper pruning."

Although nearly everyone is pleased to see the house finch in the East, it must be admitted that the bird has its faults. It is somewhat too much of a bud pruner. One winter a flock that was being fed generously on sunflower at our winter quarters in Maryland took to eating buds and early flowers of fragrant honeysuckle (*Lonicera fragrantissima*). We first noticed the habit in early January. By the time the bushes were to come into leaf, it looked as though someone had sprayed them with a defoliant. Helped to some extent by mockingbirds, house sparrows, and white-throats, the house finches had methodically stripped the bushes of a large share of their flowers and buds. Fortunately no lasting damage was done. The bushes had recovered by early summer.

William Flemer III has observed severe budding by house finches on certain plants in his nursery at Princeton, New Jersey. Forsythia and flowering plums were particularly hard hit. Flower growers in California are occasionally plagued by white-crowned and golden-crowned sparrows taking buds, flowers, and young leaves. The two species are such browsers that Californians regard them almost as grazing animals. Unlike the British house sparrows, they show no particular color preferences. They are known to attack pansies, primulas, stocks, and calendulas.

One thing to note about budding is that there is no complicated problem of why some plants receive this treatment and others do not. All plants severely affected are early bloomers. It is the larger and presumably more nutritious buds of early plants that gain the attention of birds that indulge in budding. The already mentioned fragrant honeysuckle is such an early bloomer that the flowers begin to appear after any short period of warm weather in winter. Forsythia, with much the same habit, is another shrub that birds single out for special attention. But I have yet to see a forsythia whose floral display was impaired by the budding activity of birds. Still another early bloomer, red maple, gets its share of budding. Near us in Maryland, I have seen cedar waxwings taking buds on a red maple as early as November 12.

All of the flowering fruit trees—peach, pear, apple, crabapple, and cherry—receive attention from bud-eating birds. When the flowers appear, many of the same birds come back to eat the petals and other floral parts. Cedar waxwings, as they begin moving northward in spring, subsist in large part upon newly opened flowers and dried-up fruits from last year's harvest. Competing with the waxwings, and such other flower eaters as house finches and house sparrows, are the grosbeaks and cardinals. The large, sharp-edged beaks of these birds, so efficient for opening hard seeds, are also good tools for plucking flowers and buds. I have seen evening grosbeaks in American elms eating, in almost the same mouthful, buds, blossoms, and newly formed seeds. Orioles, which will be winging their way northward at about the same time as the waxwings, are also often seen at flowers of many sorts. Like hummingbirds, their purpose is to gather nectar and small insects, which they normally do without eating the flower itself.

Leaf buds are on the menu of many flower- and bud-eating birds. Perhaps not as nutritious as flower buds, they are nevertheless eaten to some extent by bullfinches in England, and, on our side of the Atlantic, by house finches, pine grosbeaks, and other members of the finch family. House finches vary their vegetarian diet in winter with leaf buds of such plants as fragrant honeysuckle, lilac, and apple, while white-crowned sparrows seem partial to the early leaf buds of willow.

The total amount of buds of all kinds that birds eat must be enormous. This is one way that an otherwise little-utilized resource of nature finds its way into a food chain. The advantage for birds is that they have an added source of food during the scarce period of winter and early spring. Buds are one food that is never in short supply.

## Sap

Although the usual foods they depend upon may be in short supply, early-spring migrants can almost always find a source of liquid refreshment. This is sap that is beginning to well up in trees and other woody plants and is oozing from broken limbs and freshly worked sapsucker holes. Nutritious and often pleasant-tasting, the sap is in such demand that a fair share of the forest community competes for it. William L. Foster and James Tate, Jr., writing in a 1966 issue of *The Living Bird*, told of encountering no less than twenty bird (besides sapsuckers), six mammal, and seventeen insect species coming to sapsucker diggings in a woodland study area in Michigan. The writers observed the same social hierarchies among competing species that are seen at feeding stations. A few high-ranking species made others wait their turn, while even the sapsuckers themselves had to wait while red squirrels were feeding.

Sapsuckers, the yellow-bellied and Williamson's in the West, are the only two North American woodpeckers that make a habit of drilling small holes, about the size of pencil erasers, in trunks and branches of trees. Very rarely, downy and hairy woodpeckers drill these holes. With the sapsuckers, it is a daily occupation related to their chief sources of food. The holes are drilled primarily for sap and a jellylike substance immediately under the bark known as cambium. The birds also consume any small insects that they can easily catch near the holes or that sometimes drown in the sap. Sometimes sapsuckers overindulge in sap that has begun to ferment.

The government biologist W. L. McAtee, who conducted so many studies of the food habits of birds early in this century, listed no less than 277 tree species and six woody vines that sapsuckers drill into for their special fare.* High on the list of sapsucker favorites are prize ornamentals and fruit trees.

---

* W. L. McAtee, *Woodpeckers in Relation to Trees and Wood Products* (Washington, D.C.: U. S. Dept. of Agric., Biol. Surv. Bull. no. 39, 1911).

The rings of small holes they drill around trunks of trees have almost the same effect as girdling a tree. Damage is most severe on trees close to nest sites and wherever the birds settle to spend the winter. Sapsuckers breed in mountain forests and the north woods of this country and Canada; in the fall birds migrate southward, with the main winter range of the abundant yellow-bellied sapsucker extending from our southern states well into Central America.

Anyone who has tasted sap knows that the sap of plants can vary in taste from pleasant-tasting to insipid to vile. Every large group of trees, including oaks, pines, hickories, elms, maples, and birches, receives its quota of sapsucker holes. In Florida I've found sapsucker work in such diverse plants as Australian pines, silk oaks, coconuts, Brazilian pepper, and mangroves. In West Palm Beach, both sapsuckers and red-bellied woodpeckers shared sap from holes in banana stalks—these drilled by the ever exploratory sapsuckers.

The introduced trees seem to be more tempting to sapsuckers than native species. Almost always it is the same few trees that are attacked year after year. Neighboring trees of the same species are frequently left untouched. There is evidence that sapsuckers chiefly attack trees that have been weakened or damaged in some way. Among the few trees that escape sapsucker treatment are those with bark so smooth that the birds cannot get a grip with their clawed toes. Beech bark is generally too smooth for them, and in Florida I once saw a sapsucker unsuccessfully try to alight on the glazelike surface of a royal palm trunk. Even the sap of poison ivy is not too blistering for the sapsucker's apparently impervious digestion. In the swamps of South Carolina, I've seen woody trunks of poison ivy riddled with sapsucker holes.

Other birds do not share the sapsucker's catholic tastes for drink of any kind. Their taste buds not quite so dulled, birds like chickadees, most woodpeckers, and warblers come chiefly to birches, maples, hickories, elms, willows, and sweet gum for the often sweet sap that these trees yield. Sap-sampling by other birds may begin on warm days in winter when the sap of some trees begins to flow under the stimulus of warm weather.

In Virginia, as early as mid-February, sap beginning to flow from neat parallel rows of holes drilled in the trunk and branches of a sugar maple near my feeding station began to be sampled by a surprising number of birds. At first I thought a downy woodpecker was responsible for making the holes. One was busily enlarging holes and making a few new ones. But soon the villain of the piece, if that was a suitable term, appeared. Sap glistening from its bill and going to each hole in a businesslike manner was a yellow-bellied sapsucker. It soon chased off the downy woodpecker and began drilling still more holes. The New England ornithologist Edward Howe Forbush pointed out many years ago that the downy sometimes on its own drilled holes for sap. This it does, as I had observed, but its efforts can hardly be compared to the determined work of the sapsucker, which goes on almost unceasingly the year round.

Even in February, birds were neglecting my sunflower and suet mixes to imbibe freely at the sap wells in the nearby maple. Besides downy woodpeckers, the sap was luring away Carolina chickadees, white-breasted nuthatches, white-throated sparrows, and house sparrows—all of them my staunchest customers. In addition, two species appeared that hadn't been tempted by any of my foods. Darting to the holes to sample the sap, when there was a lull in activity, were a yellow-rumped warbler and a golden-crowned kinglet. The sap feeding all but

*A sapsucker waits while a red squirrel dines at its sap wells in a maple tree.*

ceased on colder days, and presumably the sapsucker was now relying more on other foods, including berries on a nearby American holly.

The occasional sapsucker that spends the winter in Virginia and northward must rely much more on fruits and berries than birds that go farther south. A sapsucker was eating our American holly berries as early as November 22, and, at about the same time, fruits of greenbrier (*Smilax*). A sapsucker that wintered successfully in Maine apparently lived on frozen apples. The northward-wintering sapsucker has discovered, however, that sap is sometimes obtainable in cold weather at wells drilled in maples at a level of only a foot or two from the ground. On some of the coldest winter days, I have seen a sapsucker, feathers fluffed out, at its lowest holes on the sunny side of a tree trunk. Cold holds no terror for these birds so long as food can be found. The bird that wintered in Maine was said to have survived temperatures as low as 32 degrees below zero!

Sapsuckers, through their sap wells, have been conferring benefits upon other birds for untold centuries. They are the originators of the bird-feeding station. Many times, especially in spring and during cold wet spells in summer, sapsuckers provide the only source of food that is readily available to other birds. Ruby-throated hummingbirds time their spring migration into the still-leafless, wintry northlands not to coincide with early wildflowers, but sap flowing from sapsucker diggings. Only later will the flowers they most depend upon come into bloom. Warblers and other small birds become dependent upon sapsuckers when flying insects are unavailable. To a surprising degree, liquid food provided by sapsuckers complements the more hearty fare we supply at our feeding stations. The services that sapsuckers render should make us feel more kindly toward this droll, sometimes destructive bird.

# Survivors in the Snow | 8

A winter snowstorm, followed by still more snow and cold, and the final calamity, icing, can be about as devastating to birdlife as any form the weather can take. This is particularly true in our middle and southern states, where birds are not so well acclimated to hard winter weather as birds in the North.

Returns to the bitter winters of the last century still occur at infrequent intervals. The heavy losses to birdlife that come during these winters should not give us too gloomy a picture of the ability of birds to look out for themselves. It should be remembered that after a series of mild winters, bird populations become abnormally high and many species will have extended their ranges dangerously far north. Most losses occur among birds that responded overly well to previous mild winters. In a sense, the occasional hard winter restores the bird population to a level that is consistent with the realities of the climate.

The same population buildups and leveling off with hard winters occur in Europe. Taking England as an example, its normally mild winters favor a high bird population. But when there is a return to a hard winter, reminiscent of the last century, losses to birdlife are apt to be very high. The winter of 1962–1963, with its unprecedented cold and snow, was a particularly difficult one for birdlife. But thanks to bird feeding and the ability of many birds to adapt to frigid conditions, losses were not intolerable. Bruce Campbell, in an article in the winter issue of *The Countryman* for 1963, describes how birds fared during this bad winter. He provides such an excellent account that I shall be referring to some of his findings. Also I have used the title of his article for the heading of this chapter. But first a word about bird feeding in Britain. This subject bears so importantly on survival of birds in winter that it seems appropriate to tell how our British friends go about it.

### Bird feeding in Britain

The custom on the other side of the Atlantic apparently originated with monks during early monastic days. During this century, bird feeding became a universal pastime, with almost certainly more people participating in terms of the population than in this country. There are differences in foods and techniques between the two sides of the Atlantic, but the objectives are the same. People feed birds to help them, and, equally important, they enjoy this close tie with nature.

Bird feeding is a more informal operation in Britain than in this country. The feeder is apt to be a homemade structure on which scraps and other foods

*A woven mesh bag filled with shelled peanuts makes a popular bird feeder in England. Here a blue titmouse is clinging to such a feeder.*

are placed. One or more mesh bags holding shelled peanuts may dangle nearby. Suet and other fats are commonly offered, and in much the same way as in this country. Food is also scattered on the ground.

As an experiment when visiting England, I tried the mesh-bag peanut feeder in a variety of places, including yards and city parks. Wherever I suspended a bag from a convenient tree limb, I was quickly rewarded by visits from several species of titmice and greenfinches. I soon had the impression that these birds were lurking everywhere, waiting only for someone to feed them.

Britain is blessed with more titmice than we are. We call many of ours chickadees. The two common species found everywhere throughout the British Isles are the blue and great titmouse. These two inquisitive, bold species are at every bird feeder and freely enter houses. Four other titmouse species also patronize bird feeders. The greenfinch, a greenish sparrow-sized bird, is not far behind the titmice in coming to bird feeders. So eager are greenfinches for shelled peanuts that they appear at this food almost as soon as it is offered. Their quick response reminded me of the way goldfinches come to thistle (niger) in this country.

Few yards are without the all-black thrush with a yellow bill that the British call the blackbird. Like the English robin, it is a bird dear to the hearts of the British. Both the English robin and the blackbird come running or flying when food is offered at a backyard feeder or bench in a city park. Chaffinches are apt to appear, too, if any are in the vicinity. A colorful, fearless bird, the chaffinch is the common finch of the British Isles. Like many of our finches, it is a gregarious bird, traveling in large flocks.

If it weren't for its slender, pointed bill, the hedge sparrow could easily be mistaken for a rather sleek-looking house sparrow. Not a sparrow at all but an accentor belonging to the family *Prunellidae*, this solitary bird of dense shrubbery is forward in one respect—it readily comes to food tossed on the ground. It will eat almost anything at the bird feeder, including crumbled cornflakes and peas in the form of lentils.

The collared dove, which arrived from the continent around 1950, has spread far and wide and is now a common visitor at many bird feeders. The British, what with their many feral domestic pigeons and larger, more voracious wood pigeons, were not eager to welcome the newcomer. But most people do not object to this small, rather dainty dove with its pleasing cooing.

House sparrows and starlings, if anything, seem more common than with us. The British seem reconciled to their presence, and, I suspect, may somewhat enjoy having them. The fact that both species are native to the British Isles is no doubt a factor in their favor.

If there is any intruder that the British do not like, it is our gray squirrel, which is an introduced animal and reportedly more destructive in its adopted land than it is with us. Its main offense seems to be damage to trees and shrubbery. It is not common enough to be much of a problem at bird feeders.

About fifty bird species come regularly to feeders in Britain and another twenty pay occasional visits. Mammal guests are uncommon, although some people cater to the hedgehog, a bristly but harmless animal that is fond of milk. During the course of the year, fifteen to twenty bird species are about the average at feeders located in the suburbs. Most are permanent residents. We in this country owe our somewhat greater variety to population changes that occur with the seasons. Water, as with us, is an important attractant and brings additional species.

The British, by making good use of household scraps, tend to offer a more varied and economical menu than we do. Moderate use is made of millet, canary seed, and hemp and flax seeds. On the other hand, sunflower and grains, including corn, are little used. Thistle, so far as I could learn, is reserved only for cage birds. Peanuts are *the* food at most bird feeders and take the place of seeds and grain. Offered in the shell or hulled, they are a favorite with most birds. Fats, in the form of suet or suet mixes, are used to about the same extent as in this country. The coconut, the meat serving as food and the hull as a feeder, is a common sight in yards where birds are fed. Tons of bakery products, consisting largely of stale bread, toast, and rolls, appear daily in yards and at waterfowl feeding places. Perhaps the *pièce de résistance* at bird feeders is cheese. All birds seem to like it and many are willing to come to the hand or fly into houses for this treat.

The birds, on their part, do not always wait to be fed. Many, with little or no encouragement, come freely into houses through open doors and windows. The titmice pay visits, not only to search for food, but, as will be described in the next chapter, to commit minor depredations. Outdoor eating places invariably have a retinue of waiting birds that seek handouts or fallen scraps. The house sparrow, unlike the nervous bird in this country, is the greatest beggar of all. Scarcely less bold are blackbirds, chaffinches, and titmice.

### The worst winter

The winter of 1962–1963 will surely go down as one of the most severe of the century in the British Isles. People who fed birds rose to the occasion by doing all they could to meet the needs of thousands of famished birds. One of the hardest problems to cope with was the large numbers of waterfowl in dire straits because of frozen ponds and rivers. As many as twenty thousand mute swans were given food and temporary shelter. But as the winter wore on without any improvement in the weather, the toll to birdlife became ever greater. Among the hardest-hit species, the wren, according to estimates, suffered a loss of 78 percent, mistle thrush 75 percent, white wagtail 64 percent, moorhen 60 percent, song thrush 57 percent, and lapwing 55 percent.

Species that suffered heavily—these five, as well as treecreepers, bearded titmice, Dartford warblers, and a number of others—did not respond to artificial feeding or did so only rarely. This was the reason given for the disproportionately high losses among birds falling into this category. Several other difficult-to-attract species, as well as the wagtails, became "more cooperative" as the winter wore on.

Insect-eating birds that belong to the same family as the pipits, wagtails wintering in Britain feed to a large extent on gnat larvae found in ponds and large birdbaths. With freezing weather, this source of food disappears. Luckily quite a number of wagtails began accepting bread crumbs, fats, and other scraps at bird feeders. At first very timid, these dauntless birds began to gain confidence and were soon chasing the other guests.

Red-wings and fieldfares, members of the thrush family that normally live in open country, began coming about houses as their natural food supplies became exhausted or were covered over by snow. The two species responded well to rotten or partially rotten apples. A lady in Cornwall discovered that red-wings fed most avidly upon her cat's cooked fish.

The great spotted woodpecker was another species to learn about bird feeders under pressure of bad weather. This medium-sized woodpecker, not unlike our hairy, had formerly been shy about coming around habitations. Woodpeckers are none too common in Britain; therefore it is a pleasure to see any one of the four species at a bird feeder.

Water was in as much demand as food. So impatient were birds to get to water in freezing weather that they came to birdbaths as soon as hot water was poured in to produce melting. A robin even jumped into a container of warm water as it was being carried to a birdbath! The way birds responded to water in cold weather was consistent with my findings in Virginia. Birds need water as much in winter as at any time of the year and their need is greatest when natural sources are frozen.

Another observation during Britain's severe winter was that defense of territory broke down when birds were particularly hard pressed. The British robin, a notably pugnacious bird that seldom allows an outside robin anywhere near it, was seen eating three and four at a time at bird feeders. The aloof ways of the British robin are in contrast to those of our American robin, which is also a member of the thrush family but much larger and given to traveling in flocks.

As Britain's unprecedented cold continued, birds were seen to take advantage of any warmth they could find, including that of the bodies of their comrades. Wrens snuggled together to spend the night in birdhouses or other tight shelters. No less than nineteen wrens were observed using one birdhouse. The extra warmth wasn't always sufficient to see occupants through very cold nights. Twenty-five dead wrens were counted in a squirrel's nest being used as a roosting shelter.

Our bluebirds also resort to birdhouses for communal roosting during the winter. As many as sixteen were using a nest box in Maryland during very cold weather. Like the wren in England, bluebirds are sometimes unable to survive cold nights even though they are closely packed together. Probably the record for number of very small birds roosting together goes to the pygmy nuthatch of our West. An estimated 150 were using the same hollow in a dead pine tree!

In order to receive as much advantage as possible from the sun on frigid winter days, English blackbirds, during the cold winter of 1963, were seen lying flat on the snow in sheltered places with wings outspread. The performance could scarcely be called sunbathing, which is a hot-weather phenomenon. The birds were apparently trying to receive as much warmth as possible from the sun's rays.

Starlings were seen basking in the warmth of chimneys well heated by flues. They do the same thing on cold winter days in this country. A number were seen one winter gathered about a house chimney in Missouri, turning first one side and then the other to the warmest spot. The observer was reminded of the way people turn about when warming themselves before a stove or open fire.

Warmth in the nick of time can revive even what appears to be the most hopeless victim of the cold. This has been proved a number of times by people who have rescued birds that were numb and almost frozen. In England, the rescuer in one case was a spaniel that brought home a nearly frozen mallard drake in its jaws. On the chance that the bird might still be saved, the lady of the house put it in the cool oven of the cook stove. After being exposed to a period of warmth, the bird revived. It was fed on a diet of milk, bread, and brandy.

*English robin splashing in a bowl filled with warm water*

Similar examples have been reported in this country. Mrs. Effie Anthony of Bar Harbor, Maine, found a song sparrow so dazed by the cold that it couldn't move. After being kept in the house overnight, the bird seemed completely restored and was released. Kenneth W. Prescott, writing in *Ontario Bird Banding*, tells of finding a nearly frozen mourning dove in a snowbank outside his home in New Jersey. Although the bird was at first thought dead, it was placed in a cardboard box and kept indoors. Later in the day, the bird suddenly revived and tried to escape. When released shortly thereafter, it flew away with a strong flight.

### Anticipating the weather

Much has been written about the ability of birds and other animals to sense the approach of storms or other weather phenomena. In some instances, animals do have an uncanny ability for accuracy in this regard. A cat in Baltimore named Napoleon was so accurate in predicting rain by lying in a certain position on the floor that its forecasts were published in the paper.

Birds sometimes announce a coming change in the weather by becoming more active than usual, calling more, or, before a snowstorm, feeding more. The extra feeding before a snowfall is presumably a precaution in case normal supplies of food should become covered over. Not that birds think this far ahead. It is perhaps a psychological impulse that, in advance of a snowfall, sends birds in unusual numbers to known sources of food. They sense a change for the worse and feed heavily while the good weather still lasts.

When I've tested the ability of birds to forecast the weather by watching their rate of feeding at feeding stations, I've had mixed results. On one occasion, birds at my Virginia feeding station did *not* begin eating more heavily before a snowfall. This was a moderately heavy snowfall in February. I knew the storm was coming because of weather reports, not the actions of birds. Only after the snow had been falling for some time did attendance begin to pick up at the feeders.

As a general rule, birds begin eating more ten to twelve hours before a bad storm. Their response is apt to be prompter in late winter and early spring. By then natural food supplies are largely gone and therefore a snowstorm is more of a menace. Also birds now know what to expect. Although older birds may have passed through snowstorms during previous winters, young-of-the-year must learn through experience. There is an earnestness in the way birds begin eating before a late-winter storm that is not seen at other times. Edna Koenig, writing in *The Passenger Pigeon,* tells how before winter storms in Wisconsin, "birds fire up furiously, every branch of every shrub around the feeders is crowded with waiting birds until the shrubs look as if they have suddenly sprouted great leaves which dance about in the wind."

Once the snow has fallen and the wind quieted down, feeding conditions become better than before. The snow may now be so deep that many ground-feeding birds, for the first time, are able to reach tops of weed stalks or low-hanging branches containing seed-filled cones or catkins. For mourning doves, quail, grouse, and wild turkeys, this may be a big advantage if the snow crust is strong enough to hold their weight. Snow also acts as a receptacle for fallen seeds. This is another reason why the snow so often can be more helpful to birds than hindering.

Birds may also be able to anticipate approaching cold. Len Howard,* well-known British student of bird behavior, states that birds will suddenly begin eating much more about two days previous to a cold spell. She also tells of birds seeking more sheltered roosts prior to a cold or stormy night. A lady in Colorado writes me that prior to subzero nights, all of the birds coming to her feeders, not just chickadees, start filling up on suet.

Even our domestic fowl, with their instincts dulled through centuries of domestication, retain the ability to sense changes in the weather. Domestic turkeys are known to seek out a sheltered place well ahead of a snowstorm, and barnyard greylag geese do the same. A farmer who saw his flock of geese head for the woods on a mild winter day knew that trouble was ahead. When the storm came, he didn't have to worry about his geese. For three days, as the wind howled and the snow became ever deeper, the geese remained where they were, bedded down in snug quarters in the woods. When the sun shone on the fourth day, they emerged, parading sedately back to the barnyard. They were hungry but unscathed.

---

* See Len Howard, *Birds as Individuals* (New York: Doubleday, 1953).

*Our bad winters*

Since around 1850, North America, as well as Europe, has been in the kindly grip of a warming trend. Thanks to the milder weather, a number of animals have pushed their ranges northward. Conspicuous newcomers in the Great Lakes region and southern Canada include the opossum, mourning dove, red-bellied woodpecker, tufted titmouse, Carolina wren, mockingbird, and cardinal.

The occasional return to hard winters of the past may dent these northern populations but never wipes them out. The opossum's hairless tail and ears are highly vulnerable to frostbite, and the same can be said of the mourning dove's fleshy, unfeathered legs and feet. Nevertheless, the two, as ill prepared as they are, seem to survive the coldest winters quite nicely. Many mourning doves, however, migrate southward, as they always have, before cold weather sets in.

The Carolina wren, the southerner that sustains the heaviest losses during cold winters, always makes a comeback within a few years and begins edging northward again. Its success can be traced partly to a high reproductive rate. Another aid, which it probably could not do without during northern winters,

*Domestic greylag geese returning to the
barnyard after a snow storm*

is the feeding station. To a greater or lesser degree, all southern songbirds near the northern limits of their ranges require the assistance of artificial food supplies.

The winter of 1977, the most severe seen in the East in thirty-five years, was a reminder that warming trends do not continue indefinitely without interruption. Occasional cold winters still take us by surprise and cause heavy losses to wildlife. Coming, as it did, after a series of mild winters, the cold, heavy snow and icing of this winter made conditions particularly difficult for small birds that normally find enough insects and fruits to keep them going.

Chandler S. Robbins, writing in a 1977 issue of *Maryland Birdlife,* describes the plight of woodland birdlife during this winter at Columbia, Maryland. As long as fruits and berries in the form of Japanese honeysuckle and poison ivy remained, no serious losses took place. But with the disappearance of honeysuckle berries and then those of poison ivy, many of the small birds began to suffer. The Carolina wren population was completely wiped out, while white-throats virtually disappeared. Other birds that suffered heavy losses included the hermit thrush, ruby-crowned kinglet, yellow-rumped warbler, and rufous-sided towhee. On the other hand, woodpeckers, with their ability to forage high in

trees, were little affected. The same was true of the finches. They too can find food high above the snow. Chickadees and tufted titmice, independent birds when they need to be, easily accustom themselves to hard winters. They too maintained their numbers.

The disappearance of poison ivy berries in late January, sooner than usual, represented a serious loss to a large segment of the bird population. Many species depend heavily on this food during the winter. I have found the same to be true among wintering woodland birds in my part of Maryland. Japanese honey-suckle is equally important where I live.

In the chapter on confrontations, I described how large numbers of birds came to cleared highways when other sources of food were covered over by snow. Heavy mortality and cannibalism were the unhappy results in many instances involving field-foraging birds. Smaller birds, which had depended upon Japanese honeysuckle and other natural foods, now came streaming to my feeding stations. With natural supplies depleted, they were frantically hungry. Even before I was awake in the morning, white-throats were fluttering against my bedroom window panes as if to tell me to hurry with the food. Once outside, they would come flying toward me from every direction. While the storm lasted, I was the sole supplier of their daily rations. I couldn't look after all the birds in the vicinity during this bad winter, so I concentrated on helping the regular patrons at my feeding station. Grackles, red-wings, and starlings, as far as I was concerned, would have to look elsewhere. But I didn't have much say in the matter. They came anyway, sometimes in overwhelming numbers. Often I had to stand outside and shoo them away so that smaller birds would have a chance.

Still other birds that I wanted to help never put in an appearance. Like the British, we have our share of non–feeding-station birds that are almost impossible to help during times of emergency. High on this list are tree swallows and eastern phoebes that winter in small numbers all the way to southern New England. In my immediate vicinity that winter were horned larks, kinglets, and meadowlarks, birds that sometimes visit feeders, but I failed to lure them.

Our robins are a little more forward than British red-wings and fieldfares. As long as their favorite fruits cling to trees and bushes through the winter, robins are likely to ignore our feeders. When they do come, they eagerly take a wide variety of bird foods. Proving that robins will come to feeders regardless of the weather, Mrs. W. E. Buxton of Memphis, Tennessee, plays host to a flock of around four hundred every winter. The birds have mastered every kind of bird feeder and come thronging to her back door as soon as she appears with food.

Bluebirds present a more difficult problem than robins. They are harder to lure to feeding stations and accept fewer foods. When large numbers of spring migrants were caught in an April snowstorm at Colorado Springs, the robins came to feeding stations, while western and mountain bluebirds failed to do so. As a consequence, many of the latter perished. The present plight of the bluebirds can be traced partly to heavy mortality during hard winters. The same winter losses occurred during the last century and perhaps much more often. However, early in the last century the bluebird had no competition from starlings and house sparrows, adversaries that take its nesting sites and destroy eggs

*Poison ivy berries are popular with many birds in winter.*

and young. Also there were an abundance of cavities in old orchards and wooden fence posts, the kind of ideal nesting sites that are ever harder to find these days. If it weren't for the large-scale efforts being made to assist bluebirds with nesting boxes, we might be nearly without these bluest of all our blue-colored birds.

### Out in all kinds of weather

If birds can so many times come successfully through the fury of a winter snowstorm, it stands to reason that less violent forms of the weather aren't going to greatly harm them. Not only is this true, but in learning to live with the weather, many birds have become perfectly adapted to the world's harshest climates. Birds may be found living in some of the hottest, driest, or coldest parts of the world. On our continent we find boreal and black-capped chickadees among the birds that brave the frigid Alaskan winters.

The fact that some birds can endure great cold, however, does not mean that all have this capacity. Some, like the mourning dove, as we have seen, suffer from frostbitten feet in very cold weather. In birds the feet are the part of the body most vulnerable to the cold. Many times I've looked out at birds at my feeders on very cold days and found them eating in a squatting position to keep their feet warm and with their feathers fluffed out. The hardy birds that spend the winter on the northern Great Plains take similar precautions. C. E. Broadman, in a 1934 issue of *Bird-Banding,* tells of horned larks, Lapland longspurs, and snow buntings in North Dakota lying on their sides in the snow with their feet drawn up into their feathers to avoid freezing them. The birds also dug holes in the snow in order to escape the cold winds.

The oft-repeated statement that birds can endure the cold if they have sufficient food doesn't always hold true. Not only are unfeathered parts subject to frostbite, but a number of birds can't stand prolonged exposure to severe cold. Mention has already been made of wrens and bluebirds dying within the shelter of birdhouses or other roosting quarters. Food and shelter help, but there are limits to how much cold birds can endure.

If something interferes with ability to find food for even a day or two, the bird begins drawing on its fat reserves. Once the reserve is gone, the bird has nothing to fall back upon. Probably most displaced birds that turn up at feeding

stations in the North in winter have little left in the way of fat reserves. Their
status is likely to be near the bottom of the pecking order, which doesn't help
them either. Unable to obtain sufficient food and buffeted by the weather, they
face hopeless odds. Only the timely help of a solicitous feeding-station operator
can save the life of a bird under such circumstances.

In my *Complete Guide to Bird Feeding*, I told of a yellow-breasted chat
that survived a series of snowstorms and near-zero weather to live through a
New Hampshire winter. The extra measures that its hosts took in looking after
this bird were responsible for its survival. A brown thrasher that survived
temperatures as low as 27 below made it successfully through a Minnesota winter.
Again, this was a bird that was pampered by its hosts. But the sapsucker, mentioned in the previous chapter, that weathered a Maine winter on frozen apples
had no sympathetic help from human hosts.

One of the most amazing winter sagas that I've heard of relates to a
hummingbird that appeared at a sugarwater feeder in Norfolk, Virginia, in late
autumn. The bird's hostess, Emily V. Moore, took almost superhuman pains to
nurse the bird through the snowstorms and cold of a hard winter. During freezing weather, the feeder was brought in every 20 to 30 minutes and replaced
with one with unfrozen solution. The hummingbird, believed to be a female
rubythroat, came to the feeder every two to three minutes for a feeding. So far
as known, it obtained no food from natural sources. The bird disappeared on
March 2, after having survived five snowfalls and temperatures as low as 9 degrees Fahrenheit.

Wind alone, unless a hurricane or tornado, is seldom a lethal force, so far
as birds are concerned. It is wind combined with snow and low temperature
that is damaging. Birds have difficulty flying in very strong wind. Moreover,
their feathers may be ruffled by the wind, exposing them to the cold. Whenever
possible, they overcome this problem by facing the wind. On windy days birds
seek out sheltered places, and that is where they stay unless they are compelled
to search at a distance for food.

I measured the amount of food eaten at my bird feeders in Virginia on
very windy and on calm days in winter when other weather factors were the
same. In one series of tests in February, birds ate about twice as much when the
wind was light as they did when it was strong. In other tests the difference

wasn't quite this striking. My conclusion was that on very windy days, many birds refuse to expose themselves to possible buffeting by the wind. For this reason, they may forgo visiting feeding stations if this involves flying any distance to reach them. Burnell A. Crist, writing in a 1966 issue of *The Wilson Bulletin*, found that rain or snow had little effect upon attendance at his feeders. On the other hand, the wind did. The stronger the wind, the fewer the number of birds coming to his feeders. This rule even seems to hold at feeders that are reasonably sheltered from the wind.

Rain, unless it is a hard downpour, normally has a less drastic effect upon attendance at bird feeders than strong winds. I've had birds continue to feed steadily at my feeders during a rain heavy enough to send me rushing indoors to get my raincoat and rain cap. Rain does not fall off birds of most kinds as it does off a "duck's back." It doesn't take much exposure to rain before most of the birds we see look wet and bedraggled. House sparrows begin to look so wet and forlorn that you almost begin to feel sorry for them. On the other hand,

a few birds surprise us by looking as though they were dressed in transparent raincoats. Mourning doves appear this way in the rain, and so do orange-crowned warblers, according to Doris C. Hauser in an *Audubon* article. She describes one coming to her feeder in the rain as having drops of water, like jewels, roll off its feathers without leaving any dampening effect.

Unlike ourselves, birds do not attempt to stay dry. If it is a light rain, they go about their business much as usual. Only when the rain becomes quite hard, pelting them with drops, or, worse yet, if it turns to hail, do they seek cover. Strangely, even during such emergencies, birds, with the exception of house sparrows, rarely seem to seek the shelter of our houses or outbuildings. Rather they go to dense foliage, or, like the blue jay I watched during a rainstorm, they find a place under a tree limb that affords them some protection. As soon as the rain begins to slacken even slightly, birds return to their normal activities. The fact that they are wet doesn't seem to matter.

So long as the rain was not hard, birds came to my feeders in Virginia in

*Juncos foraging on the lawn in the rain*

normal numbers. A hard shower saw continued patronage by chickadees and tufted titmice and no further visits from house sparrows and white-breasted nuthatches. As the rain tapered off, the house sparrows returned and cardinals began to make their first appearance. A heavy rain in February discouraged all guests except juncos. The rain brought more juncos than usual. Aptly described as bad-weather birds, juncos show up at my feeders in better-than-average numbers when it rains or snows. Carolina wrens sometimes surprise me by coming more frequently when it rains. During an all-day rain in South Carolina, starlings and blue jays all but ceased coming to my feeders.

It is almost impossible to predict how birds will react during a rain. Much depends on how hungry they are, how long the rain lasts, and how hard it rains. Whatever the case, birds seem more than able to withstand a short spell of rainy weather. Our concern during wet weather should be to see that bird foods do not become damp and moldy. Food should be stored in dry, tight containers. And food should not be left in feeders if it is likely to spoil. More than one bird disease can be traced to moldy foods.

# Houses and Their Attraction to Birds | 9

Much of the information supplied in previous chapters was gathered by watching the activities of birds in the immediate vicinity of houses. As I've mentioned before, I make most of my bird observations from the window or a part of the yard. All of the information that went into Mrs. Hauser's productive studies of sunbathing and anting in birds came from window observations. The same was true of Mrs. Potter and her collaborating studies in the same field. The two go hand in hand—the house serving as a blind and the birds outside in easy view serving as the objects of study and pleasurable interest.

Having already explored many of the activities we see from our windows, I am reserving my final chapter for the house itself. This time I have literally placed myself some distance from the house and am looking back to watch the activities of birds as they come to windows, rooftops, and chimneys. Some of my observations will also be made within the house. Birds not only come to windows but not infrequently enter the house if they have the opportunity.

Although generally not thought of as a habitat, houses and outbuildings measure up just as well in this regard as lawns, hedges, and trees. More birds may use our house for nesting and other purposes than use the grounds that surround it. This is a matter that somehow has come under very little notice. The reason, I suspect, is that houses and buildings of all kinds are neglected because of the pigeons, starlings, and house sparrows that inhabit them. It is true that all three use houses almost as though they were the owners, not us. We find their nests in gutters and drains, behind shutters, on window ledges, and on chimneys. They leave their droppings and feathers everywhere and come into the house when they can. I tend to forgive them these misdemeanors, however, for the reason that I benefit so much from having them close by. They give me an understanding of bird behavior that I couldn't obtain from watching wilder birds in more remote areas. I can give the same praise to other birds that have followed suit and now live almost within arm's length of us. The older a house, the more likely that its owner will be sharing it with birds. Birds are quick to find advantages in nooks, crannies, and parts of the house falling into disrepair.

### The vine cover

The house that is partly covered by vines makes one of the best of all bird havens. Vines not only provide cover and nesting sites for birds but enhance the beauty of the house and act as insulation. To safeguard bricks or woodwork, it is sometimes best to keep vines a few inches away from walls or siding. This can be achieved with the help of latticework. Vines on houses can attract nesting wood thrushes, house finches, purple finches, and Brewer's blackbirds. English ivy, the most popular vine of all with birds, has harbored nests of Anna's, Allen's, and black-chinned hummingbirds in the far West and elsewhere has served such birds as the Carolina wren, house finch, and song sparrow. For this information on nesting, and still more ahead, I am indebted to the Cornell Nest Card Records Program at the Cornell Laboratory of Ornithology.

Perhaps I should not leave out the fact that English ivy is somewhat too popular with house sparrows. They use ivy the year round; it serves them ideally for nest sites and as a safe roosting place at night.

Clematis, popular with several nesting birds, was used by Anna's hummingbird, cardinal, and house finch. Climbing roses were favored by nesting cardinals, house finches, and brown towhees. Trumpet creeper was used by the cardinal for nesting, and its blossoms are always a great favorite with hummingbirds.

Vines also make excellent roosting cover. About dusk each evening, a male cardinal used to go to roost at exactly the same place in a clump of rose vines under the eaves of an old smokehouse at our Maryland residence. Its arrival was always accompanied by a few call notes. Perhaps the bird was telling its mate, roosting nearby, that it was about to retire for the night. At about the same time, a mockingbird could be seen entering an English ivy vine growing nearby.

When vines are partially protected by the eaves and on the lee side of the house, they offer birds an almost perfect shelter from wind, rain, and winter storms. This is where I look for birds in bad weather and on cold winter nights. At the same time, I don't overlook dense evergreens, such as hemlock, yew, arborvitae, red cedar, and spruce. In winter, the evergreens are the place to find most birds roosting at night.

If espaliered bushes are going to be used against the house or a stone wall, I would recommend pyracantha, yew, and *Cotoneaster horizontalis*. All three provide good nesting cover and bear fruits that are taken by birds.

### Chimney and rooftop

For birds like kestrels, kingbirds, crows, and, near the coast, gulls, the chimney affords an ideal perch from which to survey the landscape and pass the time until food or other wants call for activity. In early Colonial days, the chimney

177

HOUSES
AND
THEIR
ATTRACTION
TO
BIRDS

*English ivy provides good cover for birds.*

swift discovered the chimney as a perfect nest site. The swifts could plaster their stick-and-saliva nests on the inside surface and be safe from the weather and most predators. It was such an ideal site that chimney swifts all but deserted the hollow trees which were their original nesting places. The only trouble with the arrangement was the human occupants of the house, who were likely to object to the untidiness and screen the top of the chimney in order to keep the birds out. Nevertheless, chimney swifts still find access to many chimneys. They use the dark interior for nesting and, in some cases, for huge nightly conclaves in late summer as the birds gather prior to their spectacular migration to the Amazonian jungles of Peru. As a boy, I used to watch chimney swifts as they funneled into the chimney of a nearby house for the night. There was always much circling about and rapid feints toward the chimney before the birds finally entered.

Starlings huddle against chimneys on cold winter days and occasionally bathe in smoke, as I have already mentioned. But most of all they seem attracted to the black depths of the chimney's interior. Like hollows in trees, the chimney opening beckons because it seems to afford shelter, a place to roost at night, and, in proper season, a nesting site. Descending the chimney, the starling will fail to find the requirements it is looking for—only soot, blackness, and, if the damper is open, a faint light below. Continuing its descent, it may enter the house, where it will be anything but welcome.

A lady in New Jersey opened her kitchen drawer and found a very much alive starling inside. This bird had somehow worked its way up from the cellar by way of the plumbing, after having entered the house through the chimney. In the same house, two more starlings, these ones dead, were found in the washing machine. Starlings that entered vacant summer homes on Nantucket by coming down chimneys one cold winter left a trail of destruction. Battering themselves against inside walls, furniture, and windows, they spread trails of soot and left their bodies as testimony of what had happened.

Starlings are not the only birds to enter houses by chimneys. A common loon, looking something like Santa Claus, came down the chimney of a Maine lakeside cottage one summer. When living on the farm in Virginia, we had birds ranging from chimney swifts to muscovy ducks and pigeons come down our chimney. One pigeon, showing singular lack of intelligence, came down our chimney three times in one day. A metal stovepipe leading to a stove in an out-building attracted a surprising number of starlings one fall that must have been searching for roosting quarters. No less than twenty of the birds entered a closed room by way of the stovepipe and stove over a period of several weeks. I would capture the birds, band them, and release them.

It is the gutter downspout where the starling displays its greatest skills in maneuverability. A starling can work its way either up or down a downspout. It will also build its nest at the entrance, thereby stopping drainage. This is a nesting site that tempts other birds as well. As reported in Bagg and Eliot's *Birds of the Connecticut Valley,* a pair of eastern kingbirds placed their nest directly over the drain opening in a house gutter. The homeowner removed the nest but thoughtfully placed it on the top of a birdhouse not far away. The female kingbird accepted the new location and laid all but one of her eggs in the transplanted nest. However, she returned to the old site to lay her last egg. With the nest gone, the egg went tumbling down the drain and rolled out onto the ground. Episodes like this one are not uncommon when birds take to nesting in odd sites on houses.

179

HOUSES
AND
THEIR
ATTRACTION
TO
BIRDS

*Chimney swifts gathering for the night prior to departure for the tropics.*

*Windows*

Finding birds in the house is not a common occurrence. This is something that may never be witnessed in the more tightly constructed houses of today. But birds at the window can be a daily event. They come to windows asking for food or, unfortunately, they fly into windows, sometimes killing or injuring themselves. Then there is the bird that sees its reflection in a window pane and takes the image for an interloper. In these and other ways windows enter into the lives of birds and cause us to notice them more than we would otherwise.

I discuss the unfortunate habit of birds flying into windows in my *Complete Guide to Bird Feeding*. The reasons for accidents of this kind seem twofold. The bird sees the reflection of a tree branch in the window or mistakes the window for a passageway through which it can fly to the other side of the house and out again. The other reason for window strikes is panic caused by the sudden appearance of a hawk or some other enemy. Rushing to escape, a bird or flock of birds may fly into the window. We can lessen such risks to birds by making our windows less attractive to them. There is the scarecrow method of fastening silhouettes of small hawks in flight on the inside of the window. Perhaps equally effective is an array of dangling tinsel balls, ribbons, hanging bells, and the like on the outside of the window. Normally there will be only one or two windows that are ever hit by birds. In many homes there is never a problem of this kind.

Windows tell birds where we are. They look in at us almost as much as we look out at them. If the feeders are empty, they look in to remind us to put out more food. They recognize us as the source of the food and will sometimes follow us from window to window. Another stratagem is to perch near a window, look in at us, and begin screaming loudly. To further reinforce their demands, birds may begin tapping on the window panes with their bills. During the recent severe winter, when birds were so hard pressed for food, white-throats came to my bedroom window, as I described earlier, as soon as I was up in the morning. They would flutter against the panes, and once I was outside, they would follow me until I dispensed the all-important food.

Earlier that same winter, flickers were coming to the windows, but for a different reason. We were living in an old house on the Eastern Shore of Maryland that dated back to the eighteenth century. High ceilings, large windows, spacious halls and rooms made us feel uncomfortably conspicuous. To see a flicker every now and then looking in the window at us strengthened this feeling. What were the birds up to, and why were they spying on us? To make matters worse, a bird would occasionally begin rapping on the metal downspout outside our window. Warming up, the bird would commence an ear-splitting drumming that, according to the books, was to warn rivals or lure mates. This was the wrong season for mating, so we assumed that the bird merely liked the sound of its own music. The downspout in one place couldn't stand so much banging and sprang a leak through which water gushed on rainy days.

The window visits didn't turn out to be so sinister after all. Flies, numbed by the first cold of winter, were trapped in between the screens and frames of many windows. Spiders also lurked in such places. A flicker would come to the window and jab at the wire screen with its long bill. The result was numerous small perforations in the screen. The screen effectively blocked the bird from reaching its prey.

One day a flicker came to the window where I was typing on my electric typewriter. Having seen this or another bird at other windows, I thought nothing

181

HOUSES

AND

THEIR

ATTRACTION

TO

BIRDS

*A pair of eastern kingbirds accepted a second nest site after this one over a gutter downspout was removed.*

of the matter. But when the bird repeated its visits as I typed, I began to suspect a reason. Was it my electric typewriter?

I had read somewhere about woodpeckers being attracted to houses by the noise of electrical appliances inside. Mistaking the buzz for insects, the woodpecker then tries to gain entry by drilling a hole through the woodwork. As plausible as this theory sounded, I had my doubts. Woodpeckers mainly attack vacant houses, where there are no electric appliances in operation but plenty of insects. They also drill into wooden surfaces and dead trees in order to excavate roosting and nesting holes. For such a canny bird to be decoyed by an electric buzz seemed unlikely. Nevertheless, after seeing the flicker so many times at the window where I was typing, I began to put more stock in the theory. I would advise the homeowner to unplug whatever it may be if a flicker or woodpecker of another kind persistently attacks one particular part of the house. This is about the only harmless remedy I know of should a woodpecker begin pecking holes in the sides of a house. For reasons that I've been unable to determine, woodpeckers are particularly partial to the redwood siding of brand-new ranch-style houses. This is an exception to the rule that they concentrate their attack mainly on older houses or ones that have long been vacant.

*A robin tirelessly fighting its reflection in a window pane*

Birds fighting their reflections in window panes, hubcaps of cars, and even rear-view mirrors is something we rarely see, but disturbing when we do see it. Why is the bird acting this way, and shouldn't we put a stop to it?

183

HOUSES
AND
THEIR
ATTRACTION
TO
BIRDS

In most cases the bird is a male guarding territory or defending its mate from advances by a supposed rival. It regards the image it sees as a trespassing male of the same species. In a rage it flutters against the image, stabs at it with its beak, and beats at it with its wings. All in vain. The interloper fails to retreat and matches every aggressive move with one exactly like it and at exactly the same time. The conflict goes on hour after hour, day after day. Normally behavior of this kind is seen only during the nesting season. But birds like the mockingbird and cardinal that have strong territorial ties throughout much of the year may continue to sporadically fight their reflections month after month. The female cardinal, known to chase off other female cardinals even in winter, attacks her reflection just as vigorously as her mate attacks his.

Perhaps the record for continuous assault against a bird's own image goes to the stripe-headed tanager in Jamaica. According to a *Jamaica Bird Club News* account, a pair of stripe-headed tanagers took turns in keeping up a more or less continual tapping against a window pane for over two years. Bagg and Eliot in their *Birds of the Connecticut Valley*, noting how a robin attacked the windows of a home until the screens were put on and the next year continued the attacks even though screens were on, conclude that birds acting this way have lost their mental balance and are in a state of mania. I would tend to agree. Certainly so much time spent this way would interfere with a bird's ability to conduct its normal activities.

If anxious to intervene and call a halt to such senseless activity, we can remove the hubcap or temporarily darken window panes by dabbing them with a cleanser.

### Open doors and windows

What happens if doors and windows are left open, giving birds ready access to the interior of the house? We may already have an inkling from the way birds behave after making their entry through the chimney. The bird that suddenly finds itself inside our house will fly in a state of panic from window to window.

If approached, it will fly as far as possible from us, landing on furniture, shelves, and lighting fixtures. Almost never will it attempt to escape by the route it entered. If unable to shoo it out through an open door or window, we should be able to corner it somewhere. This will give us our opportunity to reach out quickly with our cupped hands and seize the bird as gently as possible. Once it has been captured, we should fold the wings back, smooth the feathers, and let the bird lie in a relaxed position in our hand with our thumb and forefinger around its neck so that it can't escape. Most birds will cease struggling if held properly. If it is daylight, the bird should be taken outside and released. After dark, it is safest for the bird to hold it in a cage until morning.

Birds are apt to get caught in outbuildings much more often than in houses. Entering by way of open doors, broken window panes, and the like, they fly about in a confused manner, seldom having the wit to make their exit the way they entered. We can use the same techniques we used in the house to effect their escape; however, a simple solution suggested by a writer to *Audubon* may be the most effective way. This man lured birds out of his garage by placing a ladder against the open door and baiting the rungs with bird foods. Sooner or later birds would fly to the rungs and make their escape. I have a hunch that the stratagem would work just as well without the food.

There are exceptions to the behavior I have described. Wrens seem able to squeeze in through almost any small opening and, as a rule, are able to find their way out again by retracing their route. Ever inquisitive and searching for insects that live in nooks and crannies, wrens are among the most frequent visitors to screened porches and interiors of houses. Several species, including the Carolina wren, are known to place their nests in cupboards and nooks in stuffed furniture. Wrens even take such liberties in occupied homes. John Kincaid in *The Birdlife of Texas* says canyon wrens, from long experience in living in caves, are very clever about finding their way in and out of houses.

Phoebes are scarcely less bashful than wrens about attaching their nests to any convenient ledge on a porch or within the house itself, if the owners do not object. A pair that nested on a beam in an old log cabin on our farm gained access by way of a broken pane of glass in a hotbed frame attached to the cabin. The parents successfully lured the young out by the same route they used.

Phoebes attach their nests, among other places, to shutters, lighting fixtures, and doorframes. A pair nesting directly over a front door deposited their droppings on the sill below. This is always a hazard when birds nest within or on houses.

The house finch is another close neighbor that places its tidy nest in the same kind of places that phoebes do. However, the house finch requires more support for its nest. Besides nesting in ornamental shrubbery around houses, it uses window ledges, porch eaves, nooks in aluminum awnings, and, always highly popular, hanging baskets with or without growing plants. About half the many house finch nests reported upon in the Cornell Records were artificial sites on houses, outbuildings, and trailers in trailer camps.

Chickadees and tufted titmice are much like wrens and phoebes in their ability to remember intricate escape routes. Bent, in his *Life Histories*, states that the black-capped chickadee is the only species able to find its way in and out of the government-type sparrow trap. This is a wire-mesh trap used by birdbanders which has a funnel entrance easy to enter but difficult for a bird to master when trying to make its exit.

In Britain, where birds have much easier access to houses because of absence of screens in windows, the titmice almost come and go as they please. People quite frequently tempt them into their homes with food offerings. The birds sometimes help themselves without any invitation. One of their most puzzling habits is to enter a house in some numbers and begin tearing wallpaper, cardboard boxes, newspapers, magazines, lampshades, and even toilet paper. The habit is explained on the grounds that titmice, in searching for food, often tear off strips of bark.

Strangely, these rampages occur most often in the fall in good weather when

185

HOUSES

AND

THEIR

ATTRACTION

TO

BIRDS

*The proper way to hold a small bird*

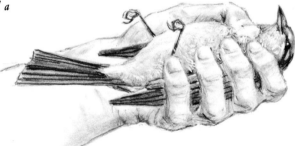

natural food is still plentiful. The invaders may entirely neglect food on shelves, but in some cases they help themselves to butter, cheese, biscuits, fish, chocolates, and sweets. They test such items as wiring, plaster, shaving cream, and candles. A blue titmouse disporting itself in a bowl of facial powder was perhaps going too far even by British standards. Like small children, the birds seem to take delight in the novelty of their new surroundings. Having examined everything and left a minor trail of destruction, they take their leave.

Frequently mentioned along with paper tearing is another habit of British titmice, as well as some other Old World birds—that of eating fresh putty and even occasionally old putty. The birds, probably attracted by the taste of the oil in putty, do a certain amount of damage to putty but not themselves by eating putty placed around window panes. The habit is not strictly confined to the other side of the Atlantic. Jean Bancroft of Winnipeg, Manitoba, kindly informs me that a pileated woodpecker came to a summer cottage near where she lives, looked in the window a few times, and then began eating putty that had recently been placed around several panes. I would expect such a habit in

*Carolina wrens have been known to set up house-keeping inside of inhabited houses.*

any one of the familiar birds that frequent our home grounds but not in the wary pileated.

187

HOUSES
AND
THEIR
ATTRACTION
TO
BIRDS

Showing unpardonable cheek, as the British would say, are birds that have learned to peck holes in caps of milk bottles to get at the contents. First observed in titmice in 1921, the habit has spread until now housewives, in many parts of the British Isles and on the continent, hurry to get milk bottles off the steps before birds can get to them. The main offenders are titmice. Other birds that have learned this trick include the great spotted woodpecker, robin, song thrush, starling, house sparrow, and chaffinch.

Habits that birds develop in one part of the world do not, as a rule, remain isolated examples. Birds in other parts of the world have a way of learning the same habits on their own. I wouldn't be surprised if some of our birds didn't take up house entering and paper tearing or opening milk bottles in the same way as the British titmice. I won't suggest that a catbird looking in the window of a room where my wife was putting up wallpaper had any such idea. Nevertheless I have seen tufted titmice tearing off pieces of bark in their search for insects. It wouldn't require much in the way of adaptation for this species to begin tearing wallpaper in the same way. Our window screens are serious obstacles, however. As for opening milk bottle caps this is a trick that was taken up by Steller's jays in Seattle without any coaching from British birds. But the habit over here seems to have quickly died out.

### The window bird feeder

As much a part of the house today as the window air conditioner or TV antenna is the window bird feeder. Of all the attractions that bring birds to our house, food is the most important. No longer are houses mainly resting and nesting places for birds. Now birds come to houses for a sizable portion of their winter food. As a result, we have vastly more birds and a greater variety than we ever had before. Even the city dweller can have brightly colored goldfinches at his window or our relatively new arrival in the East, the house finch. Well-populated districts nearly always seem to draw more orioles and grosbeaks in winter than more rural areas. In the West, hummingbirds are now winter visitors everywhere except in the colder sections.

As these and other birds become familiar with our yards, we see many staying on to nest. The hummingbirds show some of the greatest ingenuity in where they place their nests. As the Cornell nest records show, Anna's hummingbird in the far west frequently places its tiny nest on awning supports. The more widespread black-chinned hummingbird of the West nests on such unexpected places as porch grillwork and tops of patio lights. Allen's, still another western hummingbird, uses similar sites and even dangling wires or loops of rope. In many cases, the hummingbirds were first attracted to houses by sugarwater feeders. With a reliable source of food, the hummingbird population is likely to increase and with the result that more and more of these birds take to nesting almost within arm's length of us.

The brown towhee of the West is such a friendly, tame bird that it too will share our yard and dwelling with us. There are accounts of brown towhees flying into houses and then hopping about in a matter-of-fact way searching for food. Few birds make themselves so at home where man has established his abode. Californians have the pleasure of having this bird in their yards much of the time, as well as the California thrasher, scrub jay, plain titmouse, and one or more species of hummingbirds.

Besides being feeding places, bird feeders provide space for other activities of birds. Where yards are small, every square inch of surface is likely to be utilized. Therefore window trays and bird tables not infrequently become the stage for courtship and mating. No other location seems better suited for courtship feeding. As mating time approaches, the male in many species suddenly becomes very gallant and, before eating himself, offers his mate choice morsels that he has especially hulled for her. She appreciatively accepts them in a crouching position with wings fluttering. Birds not infrequently leave off feeding at the tray on a bright warm day and suddenly fall over on their side, spread their wings and tail, and begin sunbathing. Anting is seen much less often at the bird feeder, or, for that matter, anywhere. Loafing, a term for the time birds give to sitting quietly in one place doing little more than some feather preening, is another activity conducted at the bird feeder. Of course, these other activities are impossible if the feeder is crowded with birds whose purpose is solely that of filling up with food.

For a book dedicated to the habits and activities of birds away from the bird feeder, there has been a surprising amount of discussion about the feeder and what takes place there. This has been intentional. I have wanted to show that the feeder, and also the birdbath, are not the only places where we should focus our attention. We have the whole yard and house to keep in view. Nevertheless it is the bird feeder that brings us most of our birds. We owe it a special debt. The first thing I do every morning is look out and see what I have in the way of visitors at my feeders. For a more complete picture of their habits and behavior, I go to other parts of the yard and the house itself.

Unlike most other wild animals, birds permit us a glimpse of their everyday life. We see in them a mirror of ourselves although on a somewhat lower intelligence plane. Nevertheless their ways are close enough to ours so that we can usually interpret their actions. We find them occupied even more than ourselves with questions of survival. Their life is spent in evading enemies, protecting themselves from the weather, finding mates, fighting rivals, conducting domestic duties, eating, drinking, grooming. In spite of their busy schedules, they find time for semifrivolous actions, like invading our homes. There are other times when they perch quietly doing almost nothing. We see a harsher side when birds fight to the bitter end or out of necessity resort to cannibalism. We see almost demented acts like fighting their own reflections in window panes; or curious

189

HOUSES

AND

THEIR

ATTRACTION

TO

BIRDS

*Phoebes place their nests on any convenient ledges they can find.*

acts, like bathing in smoke, flames, ants, or dust. More comprehensible to us is the habit of birds, so like our own, of sprawling out and letting the hot rays of the sun penetrate the skin. Like ourselves, birds show poor judgment. They fly into windows, come down chimneys, and eat or drink foods that disagree with them.

Nevertheless, in the same, often bumbling way we do, they succeed in living out the lives they were fitted for. Year after year they rear new generations and, in many cases, fly great distances in order to meet their migration schedules. Sometimes I think birds are more successful than we are. They keep to their timeless ways and yet somehow stay in tune with the changes that man has wrought. To watch them gives us courage and a different concept of our place in the universe.

# Index

*References to illustrations are in bold type.*

# A

accipiter, *see* hawk
ailing birds, 131–2
alarms, 97–101
  false, 101–102
albinos, 132
anting, 64, **72**, 73–90, **75, 78**
  by cats, 87–8, 88, **89**
  with citrus fruits, 81
  with fire, 82–3, **83**
  history of, 74–6
  reasons for, 73–4, 76, 78–81, 88–9
  by squirrels, 88, 89
  and thunderstorms, 77–8
  *see also* formic acid
Atlantic Flyway, **7**, 10

# B

bananaquit, 18, 19, **19**
Bancroft, Jean, 38, 186
bathing:
  in air (*in vacuo*), 53–4, 84
  in ants, *see* anting
  in dust, *see* dusting
  in smoke, 83–4
  in sun, *see* sunbathing
  in water, 52, 54–62, **56**, 84, **163**
Bent, Arthur Cleveland: *Life Histories of North American Birds,* 42, 66, 107, 151, 185
birdbanding, xiv, 121, 124, 137
birdbath, 49–52, 53–71, **56**
  location of, 50, **50**, 51
bird feeding:
  in American tropics, 17–18
  in Britain, 158–60
  *see also* feeders; food
birdhouse, color of, 40–1
bird listing, xiv, 91
bittersweet, 145, **150**
blackbird, 97, 113
  cannibalism, 125–6, 128
  eating habits, 29, 30–1, 71, 134
blackbirds:
  Brewer's, 71, 107, 176
  English, 102, 159, 162–3
  red-winged, 23, 30–1, 71, **71**, 86, 97, 113, 125–6, 128, 134

# D

dickcissel, 136
dogwood, flowering, 137, 139, 140–1, **141**
dove, 54, 98
    drinking habits, 62, 68
    eating habits, 18, 19, 33–4
doves:
    collared, 159–60
    ground, 19, 34
    mourning, 23, 33–4, 37, 62, 68, 98, 133,
        164, 166, 173
drinking habits, 62–7, 68–70
duck, 64
ducks:
    mallard, 34, 127, 163
    muscovy, 178
dust bathing, 61–2, **61,** 75, 81, 86

# E

eating habits, *see* feeders; food; *also under*
    *individual species*
elderberry, 39, 142
euphonia, 17

# F

feeders:
    aggressive behavior at, 113–36
    autumn activity at, 4–8
    competition for food at, 118–21, 134–5
    window type, 187–90
    in winter, *see* food: winter
    *see also* bird feeding; food
fencerow, 137–8
    plants from, 139–43
fighting, 116, 120, 121–5; *see also under*
    *individual species*

finch:
    bathing, 67
    drinking habits, 68
    eating habits, 150, 151, 152
    fighting, 116, 120, **121**
    migration, 13–14, 143
    nesting, 185
finches:
    grass, 68
    house, 5, 29, 130, 135, 151, 152, 176, 185
    purple, 14, 15, 67, 68, 116, 120, **121,** 130,
        135, 151, 176
    saffron, 19
    winter, 116
flicker, 10, 11, 66, 68, 124, 180–2
flock, 113–14
flycatcher, 11, 55
    vermilion, 95
food, 27–48
    amounts eaten, 28–34
    bitter, 45, 148
    buds and blossoms, 150–3
    color of, 35–40
    competition for, 118–21, 134–5
    dunking, 70–1, **71**
    hidden sources of, 41–6
    "junk," 47
    and migration, 8, 10
    mistaken identity of, 46–7
    moldy, 174
    storage of, 31–4
    theft of, 31, **128,** 129–30
    winter, 143–9, 161–2, 167–70, **171,** 172
    *see also* bird feeding; feeders; *also under*
        *individual foods, and* eating habits *under*
        *individual species*
formic acid, 73, 81
freezing (defensive maneuver), 98–9
fruit trees, as food source, 150–2

## Y

*A Note About the Author*

John V. Dennis is a free-lance biologist and writer whose major fields are ornithology and botany. For many years he has had a special interest in bird feeding and woodpeckers. He is a monthly contributor to *Nature Society News* and the author of numerous scientific and popular articles. He is the author of *A Complete Guide to Bird Feeding* (1975) and, with Dr. C. R. Gunn, *World Guide to Tropical Drift Seeds and Fruits* (1976). Mr. Dennis is a graduate of the University of Wisconsin and received a master's degree from the University of Florida. He lives on the Eastern Shore of Maryland and on Nantucket.

*A Note on the Type*

The text of this book was set on the linotype in Garamond, a modern rendering of the type first cut by Claude Garamond (1510–1561). Garamond was a pupil of Geoffroy Tory and is believed to have based his letters on the Venetian models, although he introduced a number of important differences, and it is to him we owe the letter which we know as old style. He gave to his letters a certain elegance and a feeling of movement that won for their creator an immediate reputation and the patronage of Francis I of France.

This book was composed by American–Stratford Graphic Services, Inc., Brattleboro, Vermont. Printed and bound by The Haddon Craftsmen, Inc., Scranton, Pennsylvania. Typography based on designs by Susan Mitchell.